Contents

ON FEBRUARY 4, 2010, the modern-day replica of the first 2-2-0 *Planet* was inspected by renowned steam fan Prince Charles at the Museum of Science and Industry in Manchester. *Planet* was George Stephenson's next major design after *Rocket,* and ran on the Liverpool & Manchester Railway. A young Isambard Kingdom Brunel took a ride on Stephenson's world first inter-city railway, decided he could do better, given the chance – and went on to engineer the broad gauge Great Western Railway. The museum includes Liverpool & Manchester Railway's eastern terminus of Liverpool road. ROBIN JONES

ISAMBARD KINGDOM
BRUNEL
AND HIS RIVALS

C000049741

PAGE DESIGN:
Craig Lamb
Kriele Ltd
design_lamb@btinternet.com

COVER DESIGN:
Libby Fincham

REPROGRAPHICS:
Paul Fincham, Jonathan Schofield

ADVERTISING:
Craig Amess
camess@mortons.co.uk

PUBLISHERS:
Steve O'Hara, Tim Hartley

PUBLISHING DIRECTOR:
Dan Savage

COMMERCIAL DIRECTOR:
Nigel Hole

MARKETING MANAGER:
Charlotte Park
cpark@mortons.co.uk

PRINTED BY:
William Gibbons and Sons,
Wolverhampton

ISBN:
978-1-911276-64-7

PUBLISHED BY:
Mortons Media Group Ltd,
Media Centre, Morton Way,
Horncastle, Lincolnshire, LN9 6JR.
Tel: 01507 529529

COPYRIGHT:
Mortons Media Group Ltd, 2018
All rights reserved.

All pictures marked * are published under a Creative Commons licence. Full details may be obtained at http://creativecommons.org/licences

MORTONS MEDIA GROUP LTD

No part of this publication may be produced or transmitted in any form or by any means, electronic or mechanical, including photocopying, recording, or any information storage retrieval system without prior permission in writing from the publisher.

MAIN COVER PICTURE: The 1985-built replica of Great Western Railway pioneer 4-4-2 *Iron Duke* stands in the platform at Didcot Railway Centre's Brunel broad gauge demonstration line during a photographic charter on October 21, 2018. See Chapter 4. FRANK DUMBLETON

The world's most famous steam locomotive – LNER A3 Pacific No. 60103 *Flying Scotsman* – made yet more history when it entered Cornwall for the first time, on October 6, 2018. It was heading Guildford-based railtour operator Steam Dreams' 'Cathedrals Express' to Penzance via Isambard Kingdom Brunel's Royal Albert Bridge, spanning the River Tamar at Saltash. TIM SYMONS

I.K. BRUNEL

ENGINEER

1859

NEARLY 160 years after it was completed, the Royal Albert Bridge, which links Devon to Cornwall, never ceases to amaze. It was the final masterpiece completed by legendary civil engineering genius Isambard Kingdom Brunel, shortly before his death in 1859 at the early age of 53.

This bridge, like his others, has certainly stood the test of time, but if Brunel could see it today, he would immediately notice one glaring difference to his design. The illustrious *Flying Scotsman* (see image left) runs on standard gauge track, the 4ft 8½in that is normal for the British national network and those in most other countries of the world.

By contrast Brunel's bridge was designed to carry his wider 7ft 0¼in broad gauge, to which his pioneering Great Western Railway had been built. In this case, the Cornwall Railway extended the broad gauge into the Duchy.

Herein lay one of the greatest controversies of the embryonic decades of Britain's national rail network. George Stephenson, dubbed the 'Father of the Railways', had built his first and globe-changing steam-hauled railways to the narrower gauge, which was based on his observations of horse-drawn tramways in his native North East. By contrast, the more educated Brunel rewrote the railway building textbook, offering better comfort, higher speeds and greater capacity though his broad gauge.

The early-to-mid 19th century was a superior age of technological enlightenment. Inventors such as Richard Trevithick showed how the fruits of the Industrial Revolution could be harnessed to shrink the world via the medium of self-propelled vehicles.

Nobody, however, wrote any rule book which stipulated that railways must be powered by steam locomotives, or built to a particular gauge. It was left to the ingenuity of a new generation of master inventors to break one mould after another: everything was up for grabs, and the world watched in amazement during these heady times of unsurpassed inspiration and innovation.

Isambard Brunel was renowned above all others for his "impossible" structural designs, blended with neo-classical style, and the public loved him for it.

Not only did he devise a world leader among railways, but his steamships set out to extend his Great Western Railway across the Atlantic to North America, and brought about a revolution in transatlantic liners.

Brunel is now the subject of a major new visitor attraction – Being Brunel – which opened on Bristol's waterfront in 2018.

His great rivals were *Rocket* inventor George Stephenson, who built the world's first inter-city railways, his son Robert, who also excelled in building bridges, and George's young protégé Joseph Locke, who fell out with Robert and yet went on to construct far more trunk railways, including much of what is now the UK's West Coast Main Line.

In short, these legendary pioneers engineered not only trunk railways but shaped the modern world that we have today, bestowing the benefits of making journeys in a few hours, which not so long before would have taken several days.

Isambard Brunel would not be restricted to using steam locomotive haulage: in earlier times, he and his father Marc, builder of the ground-breaking Thames Tunnel, had experimented with a locomotive fuelled by gas. He would then build a coastal railway powered by vacuum pipe-hauled engineless trains.

Such experiments were certainly not his finest hour, but, as we will see in Chapter 6, a succession of engineers would follow in his footsteps in trying to develop a transport system to rival or replace the steam locomotive.

In Chapter 5, we also look at William James, who had made an early start on building a trunk railway between Britain's first and second cities, yet who had the honour and prestige of his vision and achievement taken away by history in favour of George Stephenson.

Sadly, Brunel's 'superior' railway system fell victim to the type developed and promoted by the Stephensons, and by the last decade of Queen Victoria's reign had been wiped off the face of the earth by his rivals' system, which became known as standard gauge.

However, had history taken a different turn, we might well have seen instead one of his great broad gauge behemoths like *Iron Duke* or *Fire Fly* crossing that bridge into Cornwall today.

Robin Jones
Editor

Chapter 1

BEING BRUNEL AND BEYOND

Engineering wizard Isambard Kingdom Brunel has continued to inspire and amaze generations for a century and a half after his death, and a new state-of-the-art museum exploring his life and achievements has opened in Bristol, the heart of 'Brunel country'.

It was on Friday, March 23, 2018, that Britain's newest major museum was opened on the harbourside in Bristol, one of the world's great waterfronts, at a cost of £7.2million.

Being Brunel is the latest in a long line of tributes to the legendary engineering genius who, in a BBC public poll in 2002 to determine the 100 Greatest Britons, was voted the second greatest of all time.

Not bad for a man who by parentage was half French, and was pipped at the post only by Sir Winston Churchill (a man of mixed English and American parentage).

Being Brunel is dedicated to Isambard Kingdom Brunel, the legendary engineering genius who became the figurehead of the great period of technological progress that followed the Industrial Revolution.

Isambard Kingdom Brunel's great transatlantic liner the *SS Great Britain* is the centrepiece of Bristol's harbourside, and next door is the new Being Brunel museum. SS GREAT BRITAIN TRUST

An interior view of one of the galleries inside Being Brunel. SS GREAT BRITAIN TRUST

Of course, nothing could ever equal a monument to Isambard Brunel that would better any of his magnificent feats and structures – Box Tunnel, the Royal Albert Bridge at Saltash, the original Bristol Temple Mead station, the nature-defying coastal railway route between Exeter and Teignmouth, Clifton Suspension Bridge, Maidenhead Bridge, and many, many more, last but by no means least being the Great Western Railway.

Being Brunel, which stands just a few yards away from Isambard's iconic *SS Great Britain*, is a modern new gateway to understanding much more about the great man. The new visitor attraction features six galleries showcasing around 150 of Brunel's personal artefacts, many of them never displayed in public before,

to give an unprecedented insight into his life, family, interests and creative mind, a mind and sharp talent which fellow engineers of the day sought to emulate and rival.

The age of Brunel – the first half of the 19th century – was a classic "can do" time, when the Industrial Revolution blossomed with fruits aplenty, and there were many who sought to shake the ripe apple trees.

The invention of the self-propelled steam locomotive by Cornish mining engineer Richard Trevithick in the first years of the 19th century did not take off overnight by any means. Indeed, horse traction remained the popular option as far as general state-of-the-art traction was concerned for the next quarter century, and Trevithick died in poverty

in 1834 despite his globe-shrinking invention, but such innovations set minds thinking and imaginations running into overdrive. Each time technology moved forward by an inch, its sum total would give the likes of Isambard Kingdom Brunel and his rivals an extra mile in which to experiment and explore. Each scientific nudge forward showed the world it did not always have to be the same as it always had been, but could be a better place.

Cometh the hour, cometh the men – and young Isambard was at the forefront of the global steam revolution, a man widely considered to be 'one of the most ingenious and prolific figures in engineering history'…and who would remain in competition with the best of his day.

The new Being Brunel museum as seen from the outside. SS GREAT BRITAIN TRUST

Isambard Kingdom Brunel, as painted by his brother-in-law J C Horsley in 1833.

GOING UNDERGROUND

So who was this engineering wizard? Isambard was born on April 9, 1806, two years after Trevithick gave the first public demonstration of a railway locomotive at the Penydarren Tramroad, near Merthyr Tydfil.

He was the son of French civil engineer Sir Marc Isambard Brunel and an English mother Sophia Kingdom, and was born in Britain Street, Portsea, Hampshire, where his father was working on block-making machinery.

His first name Isambard came from his father, a Norman name of Germanic origin meaning "iron axe".

Along with his two elder sisters Sophia and Emma, his parents moved the family to London 1808 when his father gained a new job.

The family were often short of money but nonetheless resourceful. Marc doubled up as his son's teacher in the earlier years, educating him in drawing and observational techniques from the age of four; indeed, Isambard had learned Euclidean geometry by the age of eight, along with the basic principles of engineering. He was encouraged to draw interesting buildings and identify any faults in their structure.

A fluent French speaker, at the age of eight he was sent to Dr Morrell's boarding school in Hove, where he learned the classics. Marc was determined his son should the high-quality education he had enjoyed in pre-revolutionary France.

When he was 14, Isambard was sent across the English Channel to complete his education, firstly at the University of Caen, in Normandy, and then at Lycée Henri-IV in Paris.

A year later, Marc ran up debts of £5000 – and was sent to a debtors' prison. However, the Government paid off his debts after Marc let it be known he was considering an offer of a job from the Tsar of Russia.

Isambard's studies at Henri-IV were completed in 1822, and he took an apprenticeship with the prominent master clockmaker and horologist Abraham-Louis Breguet, who praised his potential in letters to Marc.

Isambard came back to England later that year and soon found employment on a world-changing feature of engineering. Between 1825 and 1843, he worked on the project to create a tunnel beneath the River Thames between Rotherhithe and Wapping for use by horse-drawn carriages.

The Thames Tunnel was the first known to have been constructed successfully beneath a navigable river, and was built between 1825 and 1843. The project was funded by the Thames Tunnel Company: Marc Brunel was chief engineer and engaged Isambard as his

Samuel Drummond's portrait of Marc Isambard Brunel in later life, showing the Thames Tunnel, his greatest achievement.

assistant, over a period of several years.

Although Marc Brunel was in control, the Thames Tunnel project epitomised what would become a trademark of his son's career and engineering marvels – taking the laws of physics and nature and pushing them to the accepted limits and even beyond in his designs.

Marc Brunel had, it was claimed, borrowed from nature when drawing up the tunnel scheme, in that he mimicked the burrowing of the teredo navalis shipworm, which ate its way through timber with its hard horny head, leaving a coating around the 'tunnel' it had gnawed.

In 1818, he came up with a revolutionary design for a tunnelling shield. It consisted of 12 separate numbered cast-iron frames, comprising a total of 36 cells, in which a miner could work independently of the others, while protected from roof collapses.

The propulsion for the device was provided by a screw which drove the shield forward in 4½-in steps, the width of a brick. His workmen drove a horizontal shaft from one side of the

Construction of the Thames Tunnel in 1830.

An 1839 cutaway diagram of the Thames Tunnel.
BRUNEL ENGINE HOUSE

Inside the Thames Tunnel in the mid-19th century when it was a pedestrian walkway.

The modern-day plaque which marks the spot where Isambard Kingdom Brunel was born in Portsea.
PORTSMOUTH HISTORIC DOCKYARD

river to the other under the most difficult and dangerous conditions: indeed, the riverbed at Rotherhithe was basically waterlogged sediment and loose gravel.

The answer, as devised by Marc, was a tunnelling shield to protect workers from roof collapses, but it failed to prevent five major inroads of river water, which left several workmen dead. The first incident occurred on May 18, 1827, caused by tunnelling too close to the riverbed. There was the ever-present danger of both poisonous gases and cholera from the foul Thames water, as the river at this time was little better than an open sewer, many years before Joseph Bazalgette implemented his effluent drainage system for London.

Isambard narrowly cheated death

The Thames Tunnel was opened as a pedestrian subway in 1843 and was described as the Eighth Wonder of the World. It drew crowds from far and wide to see the first tunnel under a river. On the first day, 50,000 people descended the staircase and paid a penny to walk through the tunnel. By the end of the first three months a million people, or half the population of London, had walked through it. It was the most successful visitor attraction in the world. It was later converted for rail use. ILLUSTRATED LONDON NEWS

CONVALESCENCE HELD THE KEY

Isambard's injuries from the Thames Tunnel collapse were far worse than he first thought, and he spent several months convalescing in Brighton, during which time he suffered the first of a series of haemorrhages.

Historians have alluded to "exertions with actresses" as to why he suffered a major relapse during his convalescence on the South Coast.

Action needed to be taken to speed up Isambard's physical well-being. Still aged only 22, he was removed from

Brighton and the distractions of the opposite sex, and was at first sent briefly to a relative's house in Plymouth.

From there, he was moved on to the genteel Bristol spa suburb of Clifton in a bid to accelerate his recuperation. It was a move that would change the world.

In 1753, local alderman William Vick had left £1000 to be invested until such time as it had grown into £10,000 – and then it was to be spent on a bridge spanning the limestone Avon Gorge, which divided Clifton from Somerset.

By 1829, the investment had grown into £8000, and a committee was set up not only to raise the remaining £2000 but to hold a competition to find the best design, with a prize of 100 guineas for the winner. For young Isambard, it was a classic case of being in the right place at the right time. He set to work, with more than a little help from his dad.

Isambard duly presented the Clifton Bridge Committee with a choice of four designs, all of which involved a suspension bridge, with spans varying from 870ft to 916ft.

An engraving – The Pavilion, Brighton – based on a painting by William Westall, published in 1830.

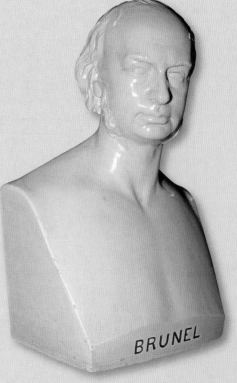

The bust of Isambard Brunel in Rotherhithe's Brunel Engine House. ROBIN JONES

The Thames Tunnel was originally designed for horse-drawn carriages, but was never used for that purpose. In September 1865 it was bought by the East London Railway Company and converted for rail use. The East London Railway later became London Underground's East London line. Between 2007-10, it was upgraded to become part of the new London Overground. It is pictured during a Thames Tunnel walk open day in March 2010, a month before trains started running through it again. LARS PLOUGMANN*

when water burst into the tunnel again on January 12, 1828. Having managed to free a timber beam which trapped his leg, Isambard found the workmen's stairs were blocked by miners panicking to escape, so he turned and headed for the separate visitors' stairs instead.

A tidal wave of water swept through the tunnel and swamped everyone, including Isambard, but carried him right up to the top of the 42ft Rotherhithe shaft and to safety. However, six workmen died, including two who had been working with Isambard when the inundation occurred.

An early souvenir of the 'Eighth Wonder of the World': a lacquered box depicting an entrance to the Thames Tunnel. BRUNEL ENGINE HOUSE

RIGHT: A scale model of the tunnelling shield at the Brunel Museum at Rotherhithe.

The Brunel Museum sits in the Brunel Engine House, Rotherhithe, in the London Borough of Southwark. It was designed by Sir Marc Isambard Brunel as part of the infrastructure of the Thames Tunnel. It held the steam-powered pumps used to extract water from the tunnel. Since 1961 the building has been used as a museum. In 2006 the museum changed its name from Brunel Engine House to Brunel Museum, and expanded its exhibitions. ROBIN JONES

The stupendous Pontcysyllte Aqueduct was designed by civil engineers Thomas Telford and William Jessop. It was completed in 1805, a year before Isambard Brunel was born. ROBIN JONES

RIGHT: Thomas Telford's Menai Suspension Bridge, as seen from the Anglesey side, with the mountains of Snowdonia in the background. ROBIN JONES

ISAMBARD'S FIRST RIVAL

The contest attracted 22 entries, and the great Scottish stonemason, canal and bridge builder Thomas Telford (August 9, 1757-September 2, 1834) was appointed as judge of the contest, which attracted 22 entries.

Telford was the son of a shepherd,

who died early in his childhood, and so was raised by his mother in poverty – a very different upbringing to that of Isambard. At the age of 14 he was apprenticed to a stonemason, and some of his earliest work can still be seen on the bridge across the River Esk, in Langholm, in the Scottish borders.

Telford set out to train as an architect, and in 1782 he moved

to London, where he met leading architects of the day Robert Adam and Sir William Chambers.

In the capital, the largely self-taught Telford became involved in building additions to Somerset House. Two years later, he found work at Portsmouth dockyard and became involved in the specification, design and management of building projects.

In 1787, through his wealthy

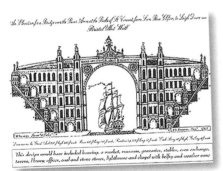

A pre-Brunellian design for a bridge across the Avon Gorge, complete with shops, factories offices, a marketplace, a chapel, stables and a lighthouse. It was drawn up in 1793 by the appropriately named William Bridges, but the plan was shelved soon afterwards when the French Revolutionary Wars led to a sharp downturn in trade and city income.

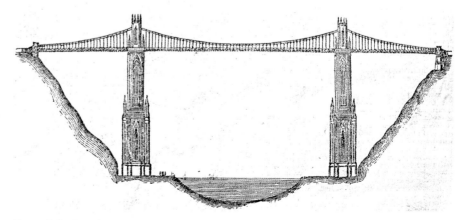

Thomas Telford's design for a bridge across the River Avon at Clifton.

patron William Pulteney, he became Surveyor of Public Works in Shropshire. There, his projects included the renovation of Shrewsbury Castle, the town's prison, churches, and bridges.

In 1790 he designed a bridge carrying the London to Holyhead road over the River Severn at Montford, the first of around 40 bridges he built in the country, including major crossings of the Severn at Buildwas, and Bridgnorth.

He did not look back. From there, his achievements were incredible. They included the awesome 126ft-high and 100ft-long 19-arch Pontcysyllte Aqueduct carrying the Llangollen Canal over the River Dee in the Vale of Llangollen, where he used a new method of construction, consisting of troughs made from cast iron plates and fixed in masonry.

He engineered the Shrewsbury and Ellesmere and most dramatically, the Caledonian Canal, and was responsible for rebuilding sections of the London to Holyhead road, now the A5.

His 580ft Menai Suspension Bridge, which carries the A5 to Anglesey and

The great Scottish engineer Thomas Telford, who rejected all entrants to a competition to build a bridge over the Avon gorge in Bristol, and then submitted his own.

Holyhead, was the longest suspension bridge of the time. Before the bridge was completed in 1826, the island had no fixed connection to the mainland and the primary means of access to and from Anglesey was by ferry across the fast flowing and dangerous waters of

the Menai Strait. Telford also worked on the North Wales coast road between Chester and Bangor, including another major suspension bridge at Conwy, opened later the same year as its Menai counterpart, which today is Grade 1 listed.

Such was Telford's reputation as a prolific designer of highways and related bridges that long before the Clifton contest he had been nicknamed 'The Colossus of Roads' – a pun on the Colossus of Rhodes, from ancient Greece – and, reflecting his command of all types of civil engineering in the early 19th century, he was elected as the first president of the Institution of Civil Engineers, a post he held for 14 years until his death.

In the contest, Telford dismissed all of the entries, including all of Isambard's designs. Telford criticised Isambard's entry, saying his bridge spans were too long – citing his own troubles with lateral movement caused by wind on his Menai Strait bridge, which was less than 600ft wide.

The committee then asked Telford

Thomas Telford's iron bridge over the River Spey at Craigellahie in his native Scotland. GORDON CHIRGWIN*

to draw up a scheme of his own, and he produced plans for a suspension bridge supported by two ornate Gothic towers set into the bed of the gorge.

Young Isambard was furious. He poured scorn on the Telford design in a scathing letter to the bridge committee, and then, his financial situation fading,

he set off to the north of England looking for work. Isambard was turned down for the post of engineer of the Newcastle & Carlisle Railway in favour of Francis Giles, who at one time had tried to replace Marc Brunel as engineer of the Thames Tunnel.

However, on June 10, 1830, Isambard

was elected a Fellow of the Royal Society, in recognition of his work on the tunnel, his plans for the Clifton bridge and his experiments with the Gaz Engine (as outlined in Chapter 6). He was also engaged on the less illustrious task of draining marshland at Tollesbury in Essex.

The exterior of the new £7.2million Being Brunel museum, next to the *SS Great Britain* on Bristol's harbourside. LOTTIE MORRIS/SS GREAT BRITAIN TRUST

INSIDE THE NEW BRISTOL MUSEUM

We will encounter Isambard Brunel's soaring rise to world fame and his landmark achievements in the coming chapters.

However, the gateway to a greater understanding of the engineer himself is now open for all to see.

The overall design of Being Brunel is set to evoke the atmosphere of the Great Exhibition of 1851 – which was a celebration of Victorian wonder and invention, and featured Brunel on its design committee.

The £7.2million project on Bristol's harbourside is located just a few metres from the SS Great Britain, the ship that revolutionised maritime engineering and world travel. The new museum incorporates the historic Great Western Steamship Company's Dock Office, a Grade II-listed building where Brunel once worked, and which has been restored as part of the project.

Visitors to Being Brunel can step into a re-creation of the drawing office where Brunel and his team worked on final designs for the *SS Great Britain*.

With tremendous attention to detail, Brunel's office has been reconstructed based on a watercolour painted by his niece, and creates a fully immersive encounter with his environment – from its sounds and scents through to the colour of the paint based on evidence found in his original office.

The museum enables visitors to discover the man behind the extraordinary engineering talent, from his unique relationship with his father Marc, his entrepreneurial acumen and design skill, through to his love for the arts and drama. It uses key artefacts and personal possessions to unravel his astonishing story.

Highlights include Sophia Brunel's diary and biography of her father – the never-before-seen diary and manuscript biography of her father Sir Marc Brunel offer insights into the Brunel family's relationships, and helps to highlight the great challenge at that time for women to be permitted to become engineers.

A glimpse into his childhood is provided by Brunel's 1821 school report and a sketch of a horse he drew at the

Inside the museum, Brunel's cigar case and the 'last cigar' offers a glimpse into his lifestyle and his workaholic nature. Very worn inside and out, it would have been carried around during his 20-hour days, Brunel chain-smoking such cigars. It holds 48 – a day's supply for him. ADAM GASSON/SS GREAT BRITAIN TRUST

An archetypal image of the great engineer complete with trademark cigar. ADAM GASSON/SS GREAT BRITAIN TRUST

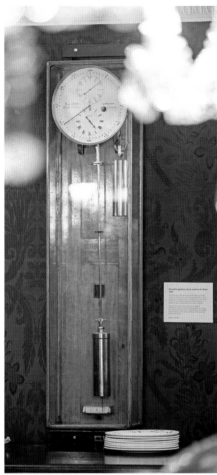

The wall-mounted regulator clock made by E J Dent of London, 1841-1845 – the clock which hung in Isambard Brunel's London office at 18 Duke Street. and which has never been on public display before. Regulator clocks were extremely reliable, and Brunel used to set his watch by this one. As we shall see, the reliability, speed and success of his Great Western Railway created the need for standardised timetabling across the UK, which ultimately contributed to the spread of Greenwich Mean Time across the UK. ADAM GASSON/SS GREAT BRITAIN TRUST

RIGHT: Being Brunel's Shakespeare room contains original paintings commissioned by Isambard Brunel depicting plays by the Bard. They were painted to be hung in Brunel's dining room in his house on Duke Street in London, and show Brunel's love of Shakespeare, alongside his patronage of contemporary artists. ADAM GASSON/SS GREAT BRITAIN TRUST

age of six – a rare insight into a younger Brunel, his talent and the upbringing that his family gave him.

Through in-depth analysis of his personal notebooks, as well as his 'locked diary', visitors will discover his dreams, ambitions and fears in a very candid way. His diaries represent a contrast to the confident public image he cultivated, and show he was riddled with self-doubt, while driven to achieve success.

His professional notebooks and sketchbooks show the scale of the

LEFT: A section of the vacuum pipe from Isambard Brunel's South Devon atmospheric railway, as described in Chapter 6, on display inside Being Brunel. ADAM GASSON/SS GREAT BRITAIN TRUST

influence of Brunel's work and how his innovations changed the face of the British landscape and informed future engineering; from his design of Paddington station and the Box Tunnel through to the record-breaking size and speed of all three of his transatlantic ocean liners.

The museum uses interactive storytelling techniques to help visitors appreciate the great thinker in new ways. Exhibits include the opportunity to board a shaking 1830s broad-gauge railway carriage, where 'passengers' will be able to compare their drawing skills to Brunel's while travelling.

Visitors can also step 'into Brunel's mind' for a multi-sensory cinema experience, where they can observe

extraordinary moments from his life as if they were seeing it through his eyes.

Matthew Tanner, chief executive of the SS Great Britain Trust, said: "By preserving Brunel's legacy in this way, the museum aims to show what the man made, and what made the man, and we aim to inspire the innovators of the future.

"It will also highlight Brunel's continuing relevance today with insight from 'modern-day Brunels', including Norman Foster and Roma Agrawal, exploring how Brunel has inspired their work."

Objects on display are drawn from the National Brunel Collection, housed at Brunel's SS Great Britain in the Brunel Institute.

Chapter 2

GEORGE STEPHENSON:
Brunel's greatest rival

George Stephenson was building steam railways many years before Isambard Kingdom Brunel set about designing his London to Bristol line, but their alternative and not altogether too dissimilar rail technologies would continue to rival each other long after their architects' passing.

Back in the city of its birthplace: Stephenson's *Rocket* on display in Tyneside's Discovery Museum as a centrepiece of the Great Exhibition of the North. RODNEY TOWERS

One of the biggest events in England in 2018 was the Great Exhibition of the North, a two-month exhibition celebrating art, culture, innovation and design, which was staged amid great fanfare in Newcastle-upon-Tyne and Gateshead.

The aim of the event was to celebrate the best of the north of England.

Culture Minister Ed Vaizey described the event as "a fantastic opportunity to promote the very best of Northern art, culture and design. Investment in our arts and culture not only benefits these sectors but drives regeneration of whole towns and cities".

The event began on June 22 with a spectacular opening ceremony, and by the time it closed on September 9, more than 176,000 people had attended.

There is, of course, much to celebrate about England's north country. However, one artefact which returned to the city for the great exhibition did more than anything else to enhance the fame and reputation of the region. Very simply, it shrank the continents and changed the world.

Stephenson's *Rocket* was by no means the first steam railway locomotive – despite an often-expressed misconception by those 'ordinary' members of the public, who are not railway-savvy.

That honour goes to a locomotive designed by Cornish mining engineer Richard Trevithick at Coalbrookdale in 1802, and of which little is known, apart from a drawing in London's Science Museum. Two years later, Trevithick gave the first public demonstration of a railway locomotive, at the Penydarren Tramroad near Merthyr Tydfil.

Still, if you carry out a survey among 'ordinary' members of the public to see if they can name a steam locomotive, the chances are that most will mention *Flying Scotsman* or *Rocket*. Such is the stuff that dreams and legends are made of.

So why is *Rocket* so historically priceless? Built at the Stephenson works in Newcastle in 1829, it appeared a quarter of a century after Trevithick's Penydarren demonstration, and 25 years two centuries ago was a fair proportion of many working people's lifespans.

The colossal importance of *Rocket* lies in the fact it contained several mechanical innovations that made it the most advanced locomotive of its day. Basically, it set the blueprint for all future steam locomotive development.

Indeed, it effectively proved beyond doubt that the way forward for the future of rail traction was the steam locomotive – and not horses. As we will see in Chapter 6, there were those – including Isambard Kingdom Brunel – who would continue to experiment with alternative forms of traction, until the day came when steam

A rear view of *Rocket* at the Discovery Museum. RODNEY TOWERS

would itself be superseded.

Part of the Science Museum Group's collection, *Rocket* was returned to the city of its birth for the first time in 150 years for the Great Exhibition of the North.

On the evening of June 12, staff at London's Science Museum began the preparation of *Rocket* for the first stage of its historic journey, carefully dismantling the wooden plinth around it and then removing the chimney, under the auspices of Louise Burden, head of conservation and collection care for the group.

On arrival at Tyneside's Discovery Museum, it was reassembled, with 18 nuts and bolts returned to their correct positions. The museum reinforced its display area in order to cope with the 5 ½-ton weight of *Rocket* by building a special platform to house it. As big a set of doors as would fit into the museum entrance to allow the locomotive access was installed; there was very little clearance either side of Rocket as it passed through them.

Rocket was displayed next to *Turbina*, the world's first steam turbine-powered steamship.

George Stephenson has been called the 'father of the railways'. While he did not invent the steam railway locomotive, he fine-tuned its early manifestations into the blueprint of what became the benchmark for future locomotive development. He pre-dated Isambard Brunel, but the pair became great rivals in establishing the future direction of Britain's railway network.

Rocket being installed at the Museum of Science & Industry in Manchester, which includes that city's terminus of the Liverpool & Manchester Railway for which the locomotive was built. MOSI

The museum also included an associated high-tech exhibition – The Rocket Reimagined – in which visitors were invited to take a virtual reality trip back to 1829 to experience the sights and sounds of the early steam age, courtesy of northern tech masters Hedgehog Lab.

Meanwhile, at the Mining Institute in Newcastle, Steve Mayes told the story of northern innovation in 40 models, using 50,000 plastic bricks, including one of *Rocket*.

Having been housed in the Science Museum since 1862, *Rocket* had received an enthusiastic reception on its return to Tyneside as a showpiece exhibit of the Great Exhibition, which ended on the day of the Great North Run.

Carolyn Ball, the Discovery Museum and archives manager, said: "It's been hugely popular. It's been one of the star attractions of Great Exhibition of the North. People have loved seeing *Rocket* here in Newcastle."

After the exhibition ended, *Rocket*, an early flagship of the Liverpool & Manchester Railway, returned to Manchester for the first time in more than 180 years, for display at the Museum of Science and Industry until April 21, 2019.

Onlookers gathered to see it leave the Discovery Museum under wraps to protect it on its next journey by trailer.

Louisa Burden said it took around

This oil painting by William Lucas shows George Stephenson seated while surrounded by his family. His first locomotive on the Killingworth Colliery waggonway is behind him. He is holding one of his safety lamps.

Food for thought and imagination: The late artist Ron Embleton's painting of *Puffing Billy* running past George Stephenson's boyhood home at Wylam. DURHAM JOINT CURRICULUM STUDY GROUP

eight days' work to take *Rocket* out of the Discovery Museum, the removal of the chimney being the most awkward task.

"After being on display in Manchester, *Rocket* will be taking up a new permanent home in the National Railway Museum in York, among other global icons such as *Mallard*, the world's fastest steam railway locomotive, and the Japanese 'Bullet Train'.

Jeremy Wright, Secretary of State for Digital, Culture, Media and Sport, said: "Stephenson's *Rocket* is an iconic part of Britain's proud railway history and it is fantastic news that it will remain on long-term display in the North.

"It is right that our great art and culture reaches all parts of the country. This bold move by the Science Museum Group will ensure more people can see this national treasure, and is an inspiring example of what can be done to make culture available to the widest possible audience."

THE ILLITERATE VERSUS THE UNIVERSITY EDUCATED

Much more of *Rocket* later, but first of all, what about the man who invented it?

Richard Trevithick may have invented the steam locomotive, which became manifested in both rail and road forms, but it brought him little fortune. He

died penniless in Dartford, Kent, in 1833, the year before the first steam-operated, passenger-carrying line in his home county opened – the Bodmin & Wadebridge Railway.

It would be the industrial North East, not the mining towns of Cornwall, where the concept of the steam railway locomotive would be nurtured, nourished and developed.

Many wealthy 18th and 19th-century investors were drawn to the huge commercial opportunities presented by the Durham coalfield, the oldest intensive coal mining district in Britain, where coal extraction is thought to date back to Roman times.

At the other end of the spectrum, the county's huge mineral wealth made it possible for Stephenson to succeed, a man who in so many ways was a diametric opposite of Isambard Kingdom Brunel, the latter having received (by the standards of the day) a very expensive education.

By contrast, George Stephenson came from a family with no money nor even the ability to read or write, but he was prepared to graft and learn, to the point where one day he had the power to change the world forever through transport technology

The Durham landscape was transformed from the late 18th

century, as colliery villages sprang up everywhere and migrant workers arrived from all over the country.

Predating the emergence of steam railway locomotives in the Durham coalfield were stationary colliery winding engines, used in the process of bringing coal from the seams to the surface, invented by a succession of steam technology pioneers, including Thomas Newcomen, Thomas Savery and more locally, Michael Menzies of Chartershaugh Colliery, near Washington.

At first used to pump out water, stationary engines later hauled rakes of coal waggons up railway inclines that were too steep for horses. The first steam-powered incline in the region was at Washington Moor, near Birtley, close to the Springwell Village site of today's Bowes Railway, now the world's only operational heritage standard gauge cable railway system.

George Stephenson was born in Street House in Wylam, nine miles west of Newcastle, on June 9, 1781.

The infant George, the second of a family of six children whose family occupied just one of the four labourers' apartments in the house, grew up with railways from the outset, for the Wylam Waggonway ran past his front door.

George's parents, Robert 'Old Bob'

and Mabel Stephenson, were both illiterate. Robert was the poorly paid fireman for the Wylam Colliery pumping engine, earning 12 shillings a week, meaning there was no money to pay for sending their children to school.

Again, here was the sharpest contrast with the young Isambard Brunel, who received a boarding school education from the age of eight and attended a French university at 14.

The Stephenson family home could at best be described as minimalist. The walls were not plastered, the floor was made of clay and the bare rafters in the roof were exposed. As a young boy, George played in the street, went bird-nesting, a passion of his father, and nursed his younger brothers and sisters – keeping them safely out of the way of the passing waggonway trains.

After Wylam Colliery coal seam was worked out, Robert senior found a new job at Dewley Burn Colliery and moved his family into a one-roomed cottage in front of the pit.

George's first regular employment was herding cows for a neighbouring farmer and ensuring they too did not stray on to the waggonway, around which they grazed. He also had to bar the gates at night after the waggons had passed by. For these duties, he was paid two pence a day.

Not the most time consuming of jobs, young George was left with plenty of spare time on his hands. With his friend Bill Thirlwall, he gathered clay from a nearby bog and made models of steam engines, even making a miniature winding machine.

The boy Stephenson was later paid to lead ploughing horses, and also hoed turnips, doubling his salary to four pence a day, but his lifelong ambition was to work for the same colliery as his father. There, he and his eldest brother James became picks, removing stones and rubble from the coal.

By the time he was 14, George was promoted to be assistant engine fireman alongside his father. However, the pit was becoming worked out, and the family briefly moved to one of the Duke of Northumberland mines, the Duke's Winning, and another very cramped one-room home.

George then went to Black Callerton pit to drive its gin horse, and at 15, he became a fireman at Mid Mill Winning pit. Two years later, this pit was worked out, and George moved to nearby Trockley Bridger, where he was employed as fireman on a pumping engine, at the 'pop star' salary of 12 shillings a week. Leaving the foreman's office, he exclaimed: "I am now a made man for life!" Little could he see what the future had in store for him.

His father then moved to a new pit at Water Row, where the engineer in charge, Robert Hawthorn, was so impressed with George's talents he gave him the job of engineman or plug-man – and so he earned more than his father.

Here, a big opportunity presented itself. George studied the machine in depth, taking kit apart in his spare time and studying its components.

George Stephenson's birthplace at Wylam is now in the care of the National Trust.

GEORGE STEPHENSON'S BIGGEST BREAK

George's golden opportunity came in 1811 when the Newcomen pumping engine at High Pit, Killingworth, broke down. It had been opened the year before by the Grand Allies, a company of gentlemen comprising of Sir Thomas Liddell (later Lord Ravensworth), the Earl of Strathmore, and Stuart Wortley (afterwards Lord Wharncliffe), the lessees of the Killingworth collieries.

After being approached by Ralph Dodds, the head viewer, while on his way to the local Methodist church one Sunday evening, George agreed to try to fix it.

Having insisted on appointing his own team of men to help him do the job, George took the faulty engine to pieces, made several adjustments and made it work better than ever before.

He was widely praised for his efforts in doing so – and soon the neighbouring Killingworth collieries wanted him to repair and maintain their steam engines too. In 1812, the enginewright at Killingworth High Pit died in an accident. The Grand Allies endorsed Dodd's recommendation that George should be appointed as the new enginewright, at a salary of £100 a year.

Regardless, George continued with his studies, now with the aid of arithmetician John Wigham, a farmer's son, at nearby Benton, who taught him to draw plans and sections.

George was determined Robert should not grow up illiterate like him, and sent him to a two-room school at Long Benton, kept by the parish clerk and his wife. When he was 12, Robert was sent to a school in Percy Street, Newcastle. Robert rode to school and back every day on a donkey his father had bought him.

Young Robert did well at mathematics, and spent some of his spare time at the Literary and Philosophical Institute and Newcastle Library.

He would study scientific books, and when he came back home in the evening, discuss them at length with his father, who himself taught Robert how to read drawings and plans.

George extended his cottage so it had four rooms. It housed the many models he had built in the evenings - stationary engines, unsuccessful perpetual motion machines and self-acting inclined planes, whereby loaded wagons pulled up the empties on a parallel track. During one school holiday, George set Robert the task of designing a sundial to go above the door to their cottage, subsequently named Dial Cottage.

Once Killingworth High Pit had been sunk, George installed his first winding engine. He also designed a pumping engine for Long Benton Colliery, and a self-acting incline at Willington, one of the first in the area.

However, like Trevithick before him, the enterprising engineer George's thoughts

The single room in which the Stephenson family lived at Wylam – a dramatic contrast with the boyhood homes of Isambard Brunel.

However, George always regretted his lack of education and his basic inability to read. At 18, he had to get others to read books to him by the light of his engine fire. So he paid to learn reading, writing and arithmetic at 'betterment' classes, three pence a week for three nights' tuition, and by 19 he was able to write his name for the first time.

George started attending a night school run by Scottish teacher Andrew Robertson, who was skilled in arithmetic. George was happy to pay four pence a week for lessons, doing his homework on a slate, again by the light of his engine fire.

When the Water Row pit was closed, Robertson moved to Black Callerton with his pupils, including George, and continued teaching them there.

At the age of 20, in 1801, George started work at Black Callerton Colliery as a 'brakesman', controlling the Dolly Pit winding gear, a skill he had learned at Water Row pit. There, he managed to save his first guinea (£1.05).

It was later said by George's son Robert that at Black Callerton, George attempted for the first time to invent a machine, an engine brake, although nothing came of it.

On November 28, 1802, at the age of 21, George married Fanny Henderson in Newburn Church, and moved to Willington Quay, east of Newcastle, where he was placed in charge of a local colliery's coal-loading apparatus.

The couple lived in one room of a cottage, and George supplemented his income by making shoes and clocks, and also in his spare time, hauling ballast out of colliers' ships.

However, at the same time, he was rapidly developing a passion not only for mechanics but the new steam technology, and in his spare time studied the principles of mechanics. George was

Dial Cottage at West Moor. BILL HENDERSON*

turned to making a steam engine that could move under its own power.

While Christopher Blackett was building locomotives at his Wylam Colliery, George was looking at them as a means of cutting the cost of moving coal from the Killingworth pitheads to the staithes on the river bank, via the colliery's nine-mile wooden waggonway.

near teetotal, preferring to save money and spend his spare time on other activities.

On October 16, 1803, the couple's son Robert was born, and he was christened in the schoolhouse at Wallsend.

In early 1805, the family later moved to West Moor, near Killingworth, George taking a new job as a brakesman at Killingworth Colliery.

Frances gave birth to a daughter, Frances Stephenson, in July 1805, but she died after only three weeks. Fanny herself died of tuberculosis on May 14, 1806. Left as the sole provider, George took a new a job in Montrose, Scotland, taking charge of the working of one of Boulton & Watt's engines in a large spinning works.

George returned on foot after only a few months, possibly because his father had been blinded in a mining accident at Blucher Pit, but also because he missed his son. Having saved £28, George paid off his father's debts, resumed his old job and moved back into his West Moor cottage. His unmarried sister Eleanor came to look after young Robert.

England was now at war with Napoleonic France, and George was called up for the army. In those days, if you did not wish to enlist once drawn in the selection process, you could pay a substitute to become a soldier in your place. George borrowed £6 for the purpose, while also considering the prospect of emigrating to the USA with his sister Ann and her husband, but he could not raise the money. Had he done so, would North America and not Britain have become the centre of the unprecedented transport revolution that was waiting just around the corner?

FRUITS OF WAR: STEPPING INTO TREVITHICK'S SHOES

In 1805, after hearing of the success of Trevithick's locomotive in South Wales, Christopher Blackett wrote to Trevithick asking for designs for such a self-propelled machine. Drawings of a steam locomotive dated September 17, 1804, were sent to John Whinfield of Pipewellgate, Gateshead, who built it at his foundry.

Reportedly running in May 1805, it was too heavy for the 5ft-gauge rails on which it ran, and it never entered service. The Wylam line was relaid with L-shaped iron plate rails in 1808.

Blackett came back to Trevithick in 1808 inquiring about a locomotive for the relaid line, but the Cornishman said he was too busy to help. It appears that by 1810, Trevithick had given up on the idea of a self-propelled vehicle, the invention having made him no money, and failed to convince those who believed equine transport was the future as well as the past and present.

Still, the industrial North East had become aware of the steam railway

locomotive concept, and it was not forgotten – far from it.

There came the time when horses were in short supply, because of the huge numbers being taken by the army for use in the Napoleonic Wars, and the price of hay and fed soared.

Anxious colliery owners worried production capability would fall and their profits tumble, and took another look at Trevithick's steamy but strange invention, and wondered if it could fill horses' shoes.

Enter John Blenkinsop, who was born in 1783 in Low Felling, County Durham.

He became apprenticed to John Straker, a colliery viewer, of Felling Hall, Heworth, and later moved south to Leeds and started working at Charles Brandlings Middleton Colliery as a coal viewer, where he directed colliery design, construction and development.

He began looking for ways to improve the working of the colliery, and to tackle the worsening lack of horses at reasonable cost. He ran the rule again over Trevithick's designs, and quickly realised the big minus point of the Cornishman's locomotives was the lack of adhesion – they depended on their weight to stop them slipping on the early railways, but in doing so broke the rails, as happened in 1804 on the Penydarren Tramroad. It is not known if Blenkinsop witnessed the demonstration of the Trevithick-design locomotive at Gateshead in 1805, but it seems probable; Low Felling was just a few miles away.

Blenkinsop looked at reducing the weight of a locomotive, but the downside was it would not haul as many wagons, so he devised a scheme whereby the locomotive would gain extra adhesion through a central cogwheel which would engage with a toothed third rail in the centre of the track. Therefore Blenkinsop invented the world's first rack-and-pinion railway and took out a patent for the design, decades before any were built to ascend the Swiss Alps or Mt Snowdon in Wales.

A trial locomotive with a small condensing engine and a flywheel, a common feature on stationary engines and Trevithick's first locomotives, may have been built around 1811, but proved unsatisfactory and led Blenkinsop back to the drawing board.

Eventually, four locomotives were designed and built by Boulton & Watt's big rival Matthew Murray at the works of Fenton, Murray & Wood in Water Lane, Leeds, between 1811/12. A license fee was paid to Trevithick because the locomotives were based around a high-pressure boiler, one of the primary aspects of his design. Two cylinders were mounted vertically partially inside the boiler to stop the problems associated with single-cylinder operation: this was a railway first.

William Hedley's *Puffing Billy* on display inside London's Science Museum. ROBIN JONES

The first of these locomotives ran light engine at 10mph during its trial run on the 4ft-gauge Middleton Railway, and then several onlookers climbed aboard the wagons for a ride.

With the debut of *Salamanca*, the world's first commercially successful steam locomotive, on the first commercially successful steam railway, Blenkinsop had achieved a landmark. His locomotives were seen as being able to replace 50 horses at a stroke, and by using them, the amount of coal carried along the railway in a day exceeded 300 tons. Accordingly, the company's profits rose by more than £4000 in less than two years. While commercial success had eluded Trevithick, the steam locomotive had at long last proved its worth.

Blenkinsop's patented system was taken up in 1813 by the Kenton and Coxlodge Colliery to the north-west of Newcastle, replacing 40 horses. One of the locomotive drivers listed there was Robert Stephenson, brother of George Stephenson.

However, Blenkinsop's rack systems

CLIMBING ON THE BANDWAGON

George Stephenson the engineer found himself in the midst of such pioneering experiments. He frequently revisited his boyhood home at Wylam to watch the locomotives steam past, including *Puffing Billy*. He also observed a Blenkinsop locomotive on the tramway leading from Kenton and Coxlodge collieries on September 2, 1813.

Realising these early locomotives were clumsy affairs that were costly to run, he came to the conclusion he could design a better one.

So, in 1813, at the age of 32, George took his idea of a new "travelling engine", as he described, it to the colliery lessees.The main partner in the mine, Sir Thomas Liddell, the future Lord Ravensworth, who had already been impressed with his enginewright, authorised him to go ahead and build it. George had to make do with the limited resources and facilities available to him

at the time, but he was determined to succeed.

In 1814, the first Stephenson locomotive, largely based on Blenkinsop principles, took shape in the colliery workshops at West Moor.

It took 10 months to build, finally making its debut on the colliery railway on July 25, 1814, when, on a gradient of 1-in-450, it hauled eight fully loaded waggons weighing 30 tons at 4mph.

Blücher, named after Prussian field marshall Gebhard Leberecht von Blücher, one of Britain's allies in the Napoleonic Wars, entered service at the colliery. It was the world's first successful flanged-wheel adhesion steam locomotive that included cylinder rods connected directly to the wheels.

While it was clearly an improvement on previous designs, *Blücher* was slow and unreliable and far from satisfactory, yet it greatly enhanced George's

A sketch of *Blücher*, George Stephenson's first locomotive.

reputation. He developed the design and in 1815 built a second locomotive, named *Killingworth*.

Over the next five years, a further 15 George Stephenson locomotives were manufactured at Killingworth, including an 1817-built six-wheeler for the Duke of Portland's waggonway between Kilmarnock and Troon.

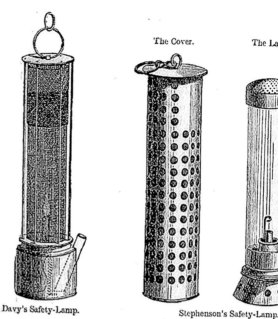

Davy's Safety-Lamp.   Stephenson's Safety-Lamp.

Rival miners' safety lamps: Humphry Davy's (left) and George Stephenson's (right).

LEFT: George Stephenson's 0-4-0 *Killingworth Billy* is now believed to be a decade older than previously thought. Built in 1816 makes it the third oldest surviving locomotive in the world, and one of only six pre-*Rocket* locomotives to survive. *Killingworth Billy* ran on the Killingworth Railway until 1881, when it was presented to the City of Newcastle-upon-Tyne, and last ran under its own power that year to mark the centenary of George Stephenson's birth. It is currently preserved as a static exhibit in Newcastle's Stephenson Railway Museum.
TYNE & WEAR MUSEUMS

were all redundant by the 1830s, rendered obsolete by adhesion-worked railways.

After Trevithick refused to build another locomotive for Wylam Colliery, Christopher Blackett asked his colliery superintendent William Hedley to build one. Using Blenkinsop's rack-and-pinion system would mean the colossal expense of having five miles of the Wylam Waggonway converted.

In 1813, Hedley experimented with a carriage operated by four men, two each side standing on stages suspended from the frame to see if Trevithick was right after all, and if sufficient adhesion could be obtained using a smooth wheel on a smooth rail. The carriage was loaded with various weights before more loaded coal wagons were attached until the wheels slipped. In doing so, Hedley proved that a sizeable train of loaded wagons could be hauled by the friction available from the driving wheels of a locomotive.

He then transformed the carriage into an experimental locomotive by adding a cast iron boiler, with one cylinder connected to a flywheel. Unsuccessful, Hedley used what he had learned to design another locomotive, built by the colliery's enginewright Jonathan Foster, with the aid of foreman blacksmith Timothy Hackworth.

The locomotive became known as *Puffing Billy*, and a name entered the English language in phrases such as "puffing like Billy-o". It regularly hauled trains of 50 tons between 4-5mph for

nearly half a century, during which time it was repeatedly modified. It retired in 1862, and like *Rocket* passed into the possession of the Science Museum, where it is the oldest preserved locomotive in the world.

REDISCOVERED IN 2018

At the same time as *Rocket* returned to its home town for the Great Exhibition of the North, one of George's earlier locomotives stole some of the limelight.

Stephenson's 0-4-0 *Killingworth Billy* – thought to have been built in 1826, three years before *Rocket* – is a decade older than thought, a new study revealed in 2018.

Latest research indicated the locomotive, long housed in Newcastle's Stephenson Locomotion Museum, is the third oldest surviving steam locomotive in the world. Only the 5ft-gauge *Puffing Billy* and *Wylam Dilly* are older, and then just by two years.

Early railways expert Dr Michael Bailey and his colleague Peter Davidson carried out a study of the locomotive and found an arrangement of components such as cylinders, valves and wheel axles indicated a build date of 1816. That would also make it the oldest surviving Stephenson locomotive, and the oldest 'standard gauge' engine.

A development of Stephenson's earlier 'Killingworth Travelling Engine', some consider it to be the first commercially successful form of locomotive. It was designed to haul coal wagons from Killingworth Colliery, where George

Stephenson worked as an engineer, to the staithes on the River Tyne.

It left industrial service in 1879 and last ran under its own power in 1881 when it was donated to the City of Newcastle to mark the centenary of George Stephenson's birth, by which time it was all but 'Stone Age' technology, having long been superseded by a plethora of magnificent machines

Dr Bailey, president of the Stephenson Locomotive Society and a past president of the Newcomen Society for the History of Engineering & Technology, has written several books and papers on early railways and locomotives, including Loco Motion - The World's Oldest Steam Locomotives, published in 2014.

He said: "The archaeological investigation was to see what the alterations were and the sequence in which they were made.

"'Billy', as we now see it, has been rebuilt on several occasions. Particular dimensions such as the wheel base indicate very strongly it was built in 1816."

Robin Gibson, railway operations and engineering manager at the museum, said: "It was Stephenson's first standard gauge locomotive that we know of, and is the predecessor of all the other standard gauge locomotives in the world."

Killingworth Billy accordingly featured in the project A History of the North in 100 Objects, part of the Great Exhibition of the North.

REFINING THE PRODUCT

A Stephenson locomotive built in 1819 for Scott's Pit railroad at Llansamlet, near Swansea, caused damage to the track, and so was withdrawn from service. George entered into a partnership with Newcastle chemist and industrialist William Losh to address the problem. They produced a series of methods that came up with different ways of fixing and jointing the iron rails to avoid dips occurring, meaning the track would withstand wear and tear from locomotives. They also designed improved cast-iron rails that did not break as easily, with these being manufactured at Losh's ironworks in Walker.

The construction of the locomotive wheels was changed from cast iron to much stronger wrought iron.

However, it was clear the most effective means of reducing track damage was to provide the locomotive with suspension, which would also ensure traction was available from all the driving wheels by having them all correctly on the rails.

Stephenson and Losh came up with a design that placed a cylinder on each side of the boiler above each axle, linked to the boiler and frame by flanges.

The top of each cylinder entered the water space of the boiler and was open at the top to allow the water to enter it. Inside the cylinder was a steam-tight piston. A rod passing through the frame linked the piston to a bearing that rested on the axle. The axle was held in a guide to ensure it moved only vertically, allowing the axle to compensate for any inequalities in the permanent way.

Nicholas Wood, the viewer at Killingworth Colliery, chipped in with his own innovation, the eccentric, which was used to operate the valves. Operated by a handle, the valves controlled the amount of steam admitted

to the cylinders and so regulated the speed.

The steam was admitted alternatively to the top and bottom of the cylinders by sliding valves, which were driven by eccentrics attached to the axles.

Poor *Blücher* did not survive for posterity. As he bettered his designs, George recycled its parts into other locomotives for the colliery. As an aside from transport technology, in 1818 George Stephenson looked at ways of preventing the gas explosions caused in mines by naked flames, and came up with a safety lamp that would burn without causing an explosion.

A month before scientist Sir Humphry Davy publicly announced he had solved the same problem – his safety lamp was to become standard equipment in mines around the world – George demonstrated his own lamp to two witnesses inside Killingworth Colliery.

The two inventions differed in that

Stephenson's lamp was housed in a glass cylinder while Davy's lamp was surrounded by a gauze screen. Davy won a prize of £2000 for his invention, while George, who had developed his lamp with the aid of Nicholas Wood, was accused of stealing his idea!

A committee of inquiry found in George's favour after he proved he had been working independently of Davy, and gave him £1000, but Davy's supporters refused to accept an uneducated mining engineer could come up with the same solution as an eminent scientist.

George's lamp was used exclusively in the North East, but Davy's lamp was adopted everywhere else. A story runs that local miners began calling their Stephenson lamps Geordies, deriving from a diminutive form of George, and the use of the name widened to being used for that of the colliers too. Eventually, it expanded to the point that any Tyneside native could be called a Geordie. An alternative explanation is the nickname dates from the Jacobite Rebellion of 1745, when Newcastle folk were regarded by the Scots as staunch supporters of King George II and the Hanoverian kings, as opposed to rural Northumbrians, who supported the Jacobites.

ABOVE: Long obsolete by the time of the dawn of photography, but by no means useless: George Stephenson's Hetton locomotive was built in 1822 and ran in service until 1912. BEAMISH MUSEUM

BELOW: George Stephenson's patented *Killingworth* locomotive.

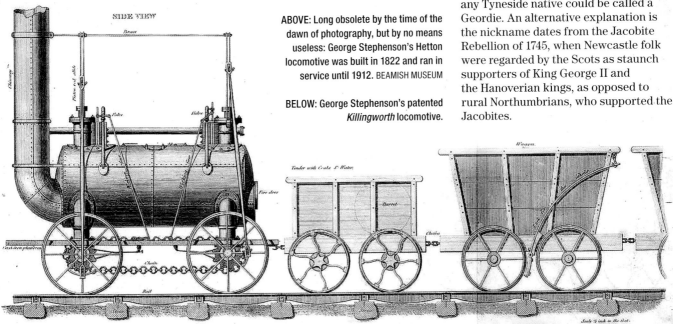

SIDE VIEW

Historians have speculated that this watercolour painting of a locomotive at work on the Killingworth Colliery railway was done by none other than George Stephenson.

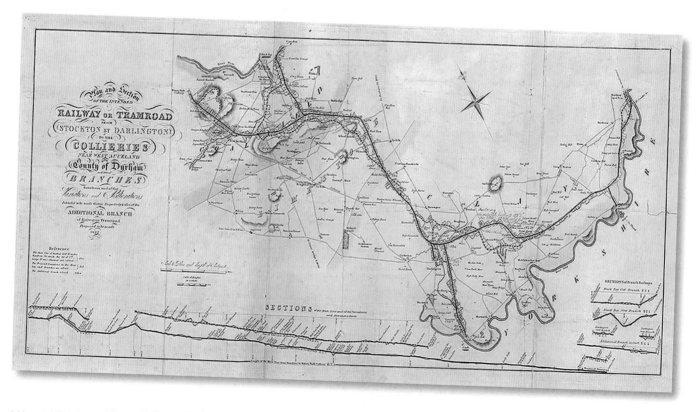

A blueprint that changed the world: George Stephenson's 1822 redesign of George Overton's original Stockton & Darlington route, which would have relied far more on horse traction and cost much more to build. NR

George Stephenson's Hetton locomotive of 1822 on display inside Locomotion: the National Railway Museum at Shildon. It was rebuilt in 1857 and again in 1882, and worked until 1912. In 1925, it led the Stockton and Darlington Centenary cavalcade of locomotives and rolling stock. In 2013, it was on loan to Beamish Museum.
ROBIN JONES

THE FIRST PURPOSE-BUILT STEAM RAILWAY

The opening of Hetton Colliery at Hetton-le-Hole and its associated private mineral railway on November 1822 has been described as the most important event in the history of the Durham coalfield.

The private Hetton Railway was the first anywhere to be purpose-designed for work by steam locomotives, and without any animal power over several sections. Not only that, but it was engineered by George Stephenson.

Before that, horse-drawn waggonways had been adapted to carry steam locomotives, often with mixed results.

The Hetton, as it came to be known, was a true first. And the man who was chosen to engineer it was George Stephenson. Aged 38 in 1819, he was a clear choice for the Hetton Coal Company, which was looking to build a new breed of railway, the like of which had never been seen before.

Drawing up the blueprint for his first railway, the most formidable obstacle facing George over the eight-mile route was Warden Law, while at Sunderland there were steep cliffs impeding the way to Hetton staithes, west of Wearmouth Bridge.

Most important of all, maybe, was

his choice of gauge – the 4ft 8in of the Killingworth Waggonway, the earliest section of which, running from Willington Square to Willington Quay, was laid as early as 1762.

In doing so, what we now know as standard gauge – often referred to as Stephenson gauge – was broadly established.

Building began in March 1821, and the line's first five locomotives were built by Stephenson between 1820-22, all of them 0-4-0s with chain-coupled wheels.

They incorporated his steam springs in an attempt to compensate for the reaction to the vertical cylinders which had caused earlier locomotives to rock excessively, but were not entirely successful.

FOREIGN ENGINEERS

Coal shipments began in 1822, and within five years had reached 120,000 chaldron wagons a year.

Other deep pits at Eppleton and Silksworth were later served by the Hetton Railway.

Very slow by later standards, the whole system was considered so revolutionary many foreign engineers arrived to gaze in wonder at it.

In 2018, an historically priceless document from the dawn of public steam-operated railways was

rediscovered by Network Rail after more than half a century. It was George Stephenson's notebook from 1822, detailing his redesign of George Overton's original 1821 route for what was to become the Stockton and Darlington Railway, and the suggested amendments to it.

NOTEBOOK 'BLUEPRINT'

The notebook was also a blueprint for railways that followed.

The 12in by 12in notebook was found by records assistant John Page in the deeds room in Network Rail's archive in York. It had not been seen since the 1950s.

Bound in its original form and written in ink with pencil annotations, it was signed by G Stephenson at Killingworth Colliery on January 18, 1822.

It contained major changes to the Overton design, which had sharp inclines, steep curves and tunnels, whereas Stephenson favoured gradual inclines and eased curves.

Stephenson also proposed the use of spoil excavated from the cuttings to build the embankments, avoiding the need for a tunnel Overton had recommended. This in itself would cut short the Darlington branch by three miles.

Overton's route relied heavily on

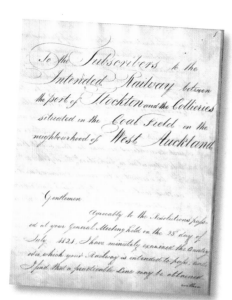

The opening page of George Stephenson's 1822 notebook.

horses and wagons, just as with his colliery lines in South Wales. In South Wales, goods would be brought by canal part way and then transferred onto wagons, which were then hauled by horses on iron tramways.

By contrast, Stephenson saw the advantage of using steam-powered locomotives and engines after successful trials on his colliery lines in Killingworth, so he replanned the Stockton and Darlington route to use them to their best advantage.

Stephenson's estimated cost for building the line was just over £60,000, as compared to Overton's estimate of more than £77,000.

John Page said: "Because it is a historical document it would never have been loaned out or requested as it didn't impact the running of the railway, so since the 1950s it has sat on a shelf

unnoticed amongst hundreds of other packets.

"I was looking for a deed for one of our internal colleagues and purely out of curiosity decided to look through the packets, and there it was, and what a thrill it was to find."

On September 27, 2018, the notebook was unveiled on display at the National Railway Museum in York. As outlined previously, George Stephenson was illiterate until he was 18, and afterwards still struggled somewhat with English.

John added: "It is said that he dictated pretty much all of his writing to a secretary. I think this is what happened in this case: it was dictated 'live', and then corrected in pencil, and then signed by Stephenson himself.

"In pencil you can see an editor has tried to 'tidy-up' his Northumbrian dialect."

THE WORLD'S FIRST PUBLIC STEAM RAILWAY

In the summer of 1818, businessmen in Stockton-on-Tees had grown tired of the decades of talk which had surrounded plans to connect their town with the south Durham coalfield by means of a revolutionary transport system, and so they had sprung into action.

Led by sailcloth maker Christopher Tennant, they wanted to build a canal which would connect them directly to Windlestone, and they set about raising an estimated £205,283, while Tennant went to London to ask Parliament for permission.

However, the men of Darlington and Yarm were worried that a slow canal with 50 locks was the wrong sort of technology. On September 4, 1818, they held a committee meeting in Darlington Town Hall in which they agreed to ask Welsh colliery engineer George Overton to investigate other possibilities.

It took Overton just 17 days to survey the area with his assistant David Davies, and he completed his report on September 20. While a canal was possible, far cheaper would be a 35-mile 'rail or tramroad' from Etherley colliery via north Darlington to Stockton, with branches to Piercebridge, Croft and Darlington.

The Darlington committee met on September 21 to consider the report, and asked two eminent Scottish engineers for a second opinion – John Rennie, who had advocated a canal between Stockton and the coalfield six years earlier, and lighthouse designer Robert Stevenson.

Wealthy local wood merchant and Quaker Edward Pease predicted a railway would yield 5% interest. On December 15, the Stockton contingent abandoned the canal idea in favour of the railway.

Edward Pease, who brought George Stephenson in as engineer of the Stockton & Darlington Railway.

The committee chose the Stockton & Darlington Railway as its name.

It was certainly not the first railway in Britain. Neither was it the first public railway – that honour goes to the Llanelli & Mynydd Mawr Railway in Carmarthenshire, which began running trains in 1803, before the Surrey Iron Railroad, which is often and erroneously awarded that accolade because it was incorporated a few months earlier. Neither can it claim to be the first public passenger-carrying line: that was achieved by the Oystermouth Railway, otherwise known as the Swansea & Mumbles Railway, in 1807.

However, the Stockton & Darlington, which opened in 1825, was the world's first public steam-powered railway, insofar as it used steam locomotives to pull freight trains, as opposed to horse traction.

It is often overlooked its first passenger trains were also horse drawn,

and not hauled by steam until 1833. The Canterbury & Whitstable Railway, which opened on May 3, 1830, provided steam-hauled passenger trains from the outset, and so pre-dated it in this respect.

The first reading of the Stockton & Darlington Railway Bill, in 1819, was opposed by local landed gentry and was rejected by a majority of 13.

The scheme was revised, routes were altered, and finally it was agreed there should be a $26\frac{7}{8}$-mile main line from Stockton to Witton Park and branches to Yarm, Darlington, Coundon and Haggerleases Lane. It was presented to Parliament in 1821, passed by the Lords on April 17, and received the Royal Assent two days later.

The line was intended to be open to the public, like a highway, on the payment of tolls of four pence per mile for limestone, road metal, manure, coal, coke, cinders, stone, marl, sand, lime, clay and ironstone; sixpence per mile for lead, bar iron and timber; and a halfpenny per mile for all coal for export. A shilling per ton was to be charged for conveyance over the inclined plans on the route.

On May 12, 1821, the new Stockton and Darlington Railway Company met in Darlington. A week later Pease brought in George Stephenson, who with his son Robert re-surveyed the route originally drawn up by Overton.

Having considerably increased his wealth by then, George married Betty Hindmarsh at Newburn on March 29 1820, but the couple had no children.

A month after he began building the Hetton Railway, George was offered the job as engineer of the new Stockton & Darlington Railway on January 22, 1822. It was George who persuaded Pease to opt for steam haulage.

The best-known work by 19th-century Darlington artist John Dobbin is The Opening of the Stockton to Darlington Railway, portraying the first train to cross one of its standout features, the Skerne Viaduct.

A scale model of the first Stockton & Darlington Railway carriage *Experiment* is displayed inside the DB Museum in Nuremberg. ROBIN JONES

RIGHT: Official notice announcing the opening of the Stockton & Darlington Railway.

THE
STOCKTON & DARLINGTON
RAILWAY COMPANY
Hereby give Notice,

THAT the FORMAL OPENING of their RAILWAY will take place on the 27th instant, as announced in the public Papers.—The Proprietors will assemble at the Permanent Steam Engine, situated below BRUSSELTON TOWER*, about nine Miles West of DARLINGTON, at 8 o'clock, and, after examining their extensive inclined Planes there, will start from the Foot of the BRUSSELTON descending Plane, at 9 o'clock, in the following Order :——

   1. THE COMPANY's LOCOMOTIVE ENGINE.
   2. The ENGINE's TENDER, with Water and Coals.
   3. SIX WAGGONS, laden with Coals, Merchandize, &c.
   4. The COMMITTEE, and other PROPRIETORS, in the COACH belonging to the COMPANY.
   5. SIX WAGGONS, with Seats reserved for STRANGERS.
   6. FOURTEEN WAGGONS, for the Conveyance of Workmen and others.

   ☞ The WHOLE of the above to proceed to STOCKTON.

   7. SIX WAGGONS, laden with Coals, to leave the Procession at the DARLINGTON BRANCH.
   8. SIX WAGGONS, drawn by Horses, for Workmen and others.
   9. Ditto   Ditto.
  10. Ditto   Ditto.
  11. Ditto   ·Ditto.

The COMPANY's WORKMEN to leave the Procession at DARLINGTON, and DINE at that Place at ONE o'clock; excepting those to whom Tickets are specially given for YARM, and for whom Conveyances will be provided, on their Arrival at STOCKTON.

TICKETS will be given to the Workmen who are to dine at DARLINGTON, specifying the Houses of Entertainment.

The PROPRIETORS, and such of the NOBILITY and GENTRY as may honour them with their Company, will DINE precisely at THREE o'clock, at the TOWN-HALL, STOCKTON.—Such of the Party as may incline to return to DARLINGTON that Evening, will find Conveyances in waiting for their Accommodation, to start from the COMPANY's WHARF there precisely at SEVEN o'clock.

The COMPANY take this Opportunity of enjoining on all their WORK-PEOPLE that Attention to *Sobriety* and *Decorum* which they have hitherto had the Pleasure of observing.

The COMMITTEE give this PUBLIC NOTICE, that all Persons who shall ride upon, or by the sides of, the RAILWAY, on Horseback, will incur the Penalties imposed by the Acts of Parliament passed relative to this RAILWAY.

* Any Individuals desirous of seeing the Train of Waggons descending the inclined Plane from ETHERLEY, and in Progress to BRUSSELTON, may have an Opportunity of so doing, by being on the RAILWAY at ST. HELEN's AUCKLAND not later than Half-past Seven o'clock.

RAILWAY-OFFICE, Sept. 19th, 1825.

ITS FIRE LIT BY A MAGNIFYING GLASS!

In 1823, a second Stockton & Darlington Railway Bill was submitted to Parliament, and included a clause allowing for the carriage of passengers by steam power. It received the Royal Assent on May 23.

In 1825, Timothy Hackworth was taken on as the first locomotive superintendent. By this time, George Stephenson was becoming very involved in the proposed Liverpool & Manchester Railway and was frequently absent from the North East, so he recommended Hackworth.

On September 17 that year, locomotive *Active*, later renamed *Locomotion No. 1*, left Newcastle on a wagon drawn by a team of horses en route for Aycliffe Lane, later Heighington station.

Once positioned on the track, its fire was lit by the sun through Robert Metcalfe's magnifying glass.

The company's official coach, *Experiment*, was delivered from Newcastle on September 26, 1825 and attached to *Locomotion No. 1* at Shildon before several directors, including Edward Pease and George Stephenson, undertook a trial run to Darlington.

At 7am the following day, 12 waggons filled with coal were taken from Phoenix Pit to the foot of the Etherley incline, where they were drawn up and lowered down to St Helen's level crossing. After a waggon loaded with flour was added

The original eastern terminus of the Stockton & Darlington Railway, also said to be the world's first ticket office, survives at No. 48 Bridge Road, Stockton-on-Tees. BRIAN SHARPE

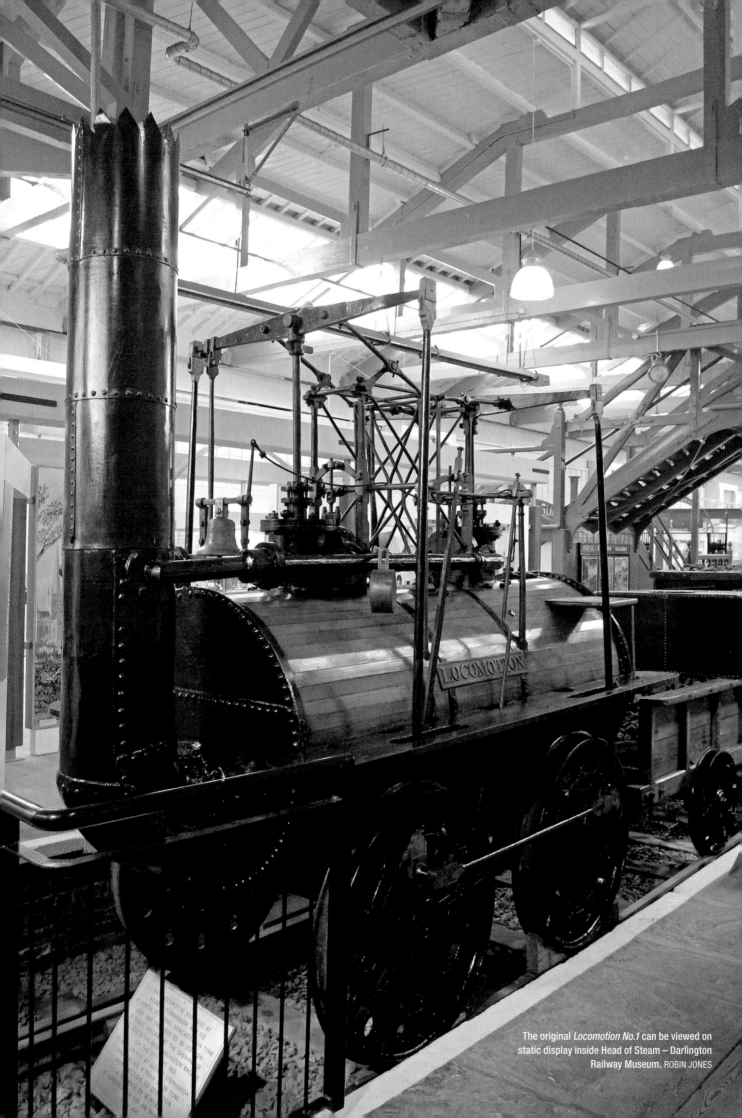

The original *Locomotion No.1* can be viewed on static display inside Head of Steam – Darlington Railway Museum. ROBIN JONES

Beamish Museum in County Durham has long been established as both the world leader in the study of early steam railways and the building of replicas. That is appropriate in view of the fact Durham is considered by historians to be the cradle of the steam railway, if not its birthplace. In 1975, Beamish staff built a working replica of *Locomotion No. 1,* the first locomotive to run on the Stockton & Darlington Railway. BEAMISH

to the train it was hauled by horse across the Gaunless Bridge to the foot of the Brusselton incline, where some passengers boarded, mainly labourers who had built the line.

A crowd cheered as the wagons were hauled up by the Brusselton engine and lowered down to Shildon Lane End (now Masons' Arms Crossing), where *Locomotion No. 1* waited in steam.

From there, the engine hauled 21 waggons fitted with seats, along with *Experiment*, in the form of a procession led by a man on horseback bearing a flag.

Despite two stoppages, the train reached Darlington inside two hours, having recorded an average speed of 8mph.

Nearly six hours after leaving Shildon, the train arrived in Stockton to a tumultuous welcome and immortalised the Stockton & Darlington in the history books.

However, by then, George was already frying far bigger fish, in the form of plans for the world's first inter-city railway.

And so it was that the world's first proper railway got its first public airing 200 years ago.

The Stockton & Darlington Railway opened on September 27, 1825, and so

The late Ronald Embleton's portrayal of *Locomotion No.1* speeding past a stagecoach on the opening day of the Stockton & Darlington Railway.

this year is its 193rd anniversary, which was celebrated on Sunday, September 30 with a party day at Darlington's Head of Steam museum. There were stalls, mini train rides, face painting, balloon modelling, a flea circus, plus street

theatre and music. There was also free admission to the museum, meaning visitors were able to get up close and personal to *Locomotion No. 1*.

Is there a more historically important locomotive anywhere in the world?

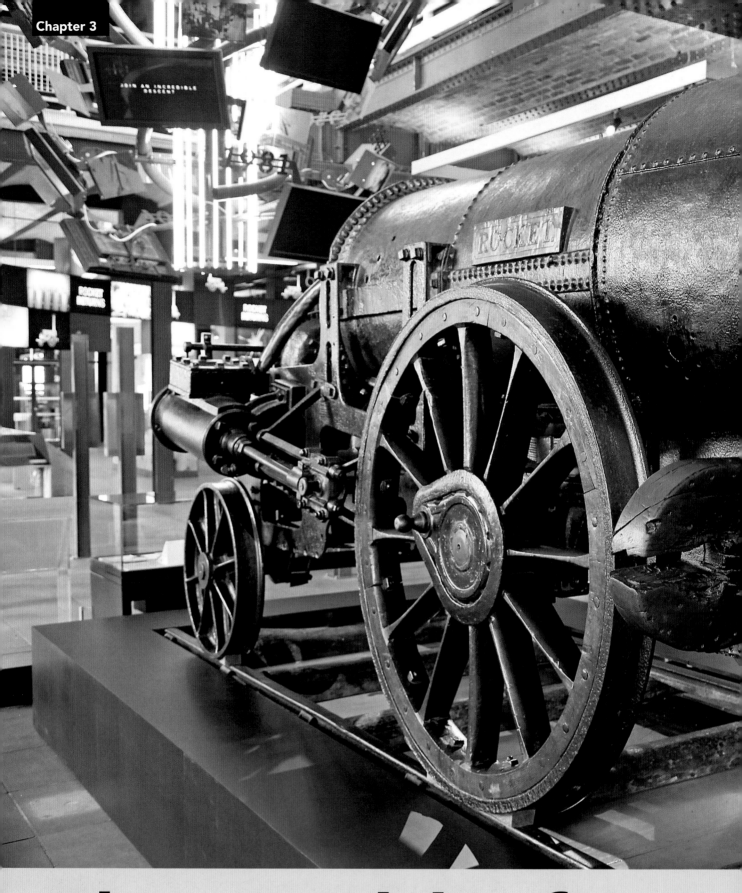

Chapter 3

The world's first inter-city railway

Back home: In 2018 Stephenson's *Rocket* was displayed inside the Museum of Science & Industry in Manchester, which includes the Liverpool Road terminus of the Liverpool & Manchester Railway on which the engine ran from 1829 onwards. NRM

While the North East is regarded as 'the cradle of the railways', Manchester has been dubbed the 'cradle of the Industrial Revolution'.

In 1761, the first section of the Duke of Bridgwater's canal opened around Manchester, sparking off a new age of artificial inland waterways, a concept first brought to Britain by the Romans.

The late-18th century canal network serving the industrial Midlands and the north country made the shipment of raw materials and bulk goods possible, allowing factories and mills to open and thrive at a hitherto unprecedented rate.

Villagers mushroomed into towns as farm labourers flocked from the rural areas for guaranteed wages in the new factories and textile mills, and where there had once been green fields, there now stood conurbations. The textile mills of Lancashire radically changed the urban landscape.

In the North West, Liverpool was the port from which finished products were exported, and through which American cotton for the Lancashire mills was imported. By the second half of the 18th century, it had replaced Bristol as England's second port. Yet land connections between Liverpool and Manchester were poor, and when the Bridgewater Canal opened from Runcorn to Manchester in 1776, it was competing with the Mersey & Irwell Navigation.

There was sufficient trade for both to co-exist, but customers became increasingly concerned at the high fees charged, and the monopoly held by the owners of the waterside warehouses, and with the proprietors owning most of the warehouses on the canal sides and river banks, a duopoly arose, with little credible alternative transport.

In autumn 1802, William James, a Warwickshire solicitor and land agent, who had already made a fortune from

The young Robert Stephenson.

The once-illiterate George Stephenson had excelled himself with the building of the world's first public steam-operating railway, linking collieries in the North East to a port. The next step in his illustrious rags-to-riches career would not only be the building of a railway to link two of Europe's major cities, but the development of competent traction to haul its trains that would set the blueprint for future steam locomotive development.

One of George Stephenson's young protégés, Joseph Locke was to become a major figure in the creation of trunk railways in Britain.

mines and a canal, visited Merseyside, and some historians believe it was he who came up with an idea to link both cities. Much more of him in Chapter 5.

In 1820, Thomas Gray published a paper – Observations of a General Iron-way – calling for Liverpool & Manchester to be linked by rail, as the first part of a system linking all of Britain's major cities.

In 1821, James visited the North East and met George Stephenson, and discussed his idea of a railway to link Liverpool and Manchester. The following year, he wrote to George Stephenson, explaining his plan in details. His railway would have a stationary steam

An engineers' train runs through Olive Mount Cutting, with navvies still hewing rock from the upper sides.

engine at the Liverpool end to haul trains by cable, but the rest of the line would be worked by steam locomotives.

Wealthy Liverpool corn merchant Joseph Sandars formed the Liverpool & Manchester Railway Company – and in 1824 appointed George Stephenson as engineer to produce a new survey for it, based somewhat on an earlier recommendation from James.

An enabling Bill for the Liverpool

LEFT: Chat Moss, one of the bleakest places on the early railway network, was a major challenge to George Stephenson building the Liverpool & Manchester Railway because of the absence of a solid base for the track, particularly at a location known as Blackpool Hole. It is believed Joseph Locke came up with the solution of building the line on a 'floating' wood and stone foundation. The first train ran over the bog in 1830, and the line is still in use today.

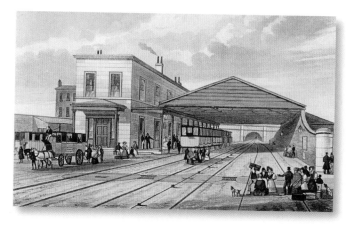

An 1833 depiction of Crown Street station, the original western terminus before Liverpool's Lime Street station was opened, and which was designed by George Stephenson.

George Stephenson's skew bridge at Rainhill station was the first to cross any railway at an angle. The listed bridge today carries the A57 Warrington Road.

The Blackburne Place ventilation shaft for the 1.26-mile Edge Hill (or Wapping) Tunnel, which was the first tunnel in the world to be bored beneath a city. It allowed freight trains to operate between Liverpool docks and Manchester, and runs downhill from Edge Hill cutting, near the former Crown Street station goods yard, to Park Lane goods station, near Wapping Dock. Its 1-in-48 gradient was far too steep for early steam locomotives so a stationary engine was installed at Edge Hill cutting to haul wagons by rope up from Park Lane good station at the south end docks. The goods wagons were connected to locomotives at Edge Hill to continue their journey to Manchester. The tunnel opened in 1830 and closed on May 15, 1972.

Another Stephenson global first: The magnificent yellow sandstone and red brick nine-arch Grade 1 Sankey Viaduct, the earliest major railway viaduct in the world. It was built by George Stephenson between 1828-30 for the Liverpool & Manchester Railway to cross the line of the Sankey Canal, with sufficient clearance for the Mersey sailing flats which used the waterway.

& Manchester Railway, presented to Parliament in 1825, was opposed by owners of the waterways and was thrown out after some of Stephenson's measurements did not tally.

Undeterred, the Liverpool committee opted for a second chance and this time appointed brothers George and John Rennie, who built London Bridge, as engineers.

They took a more conciliatory approach to the canal owners and drew up a markedly different 35-mile route. A new Bill was passed in April 1826, which received Royal Assent on May 1.

However, a disagreement between George Rennie and the company board broke out when he refused to work with Stephenson, who was proposed for the post of consulting engineer under Rennie. The dispute led to Stephenson being appointed as engineer on an annual salary of £800.

Stephenson brought in one of his own men, Joseph Locke, to work alongside him. Locke was a close friend of his son Robert and had worked under him at the Robert Stephenson & Co locomotive works in Newcastle at the age of 18.

At the Liverpool & Manchester Railway, Locke took charge of the eastern end of the line, including the seemingly insurmountable obstacle of Chat Moss, a peat bog which many said could not be crossed. They were proved wrong with a 4¾-mile crossing made possible only by sinking wooden and heather hurdles into it to provide a solid foundation.

Stephenson is widely credited for this achievement, which left the railway effectively floating on the bog, but many historians believe it was Locke who came up with the correct method for taking the line over it.

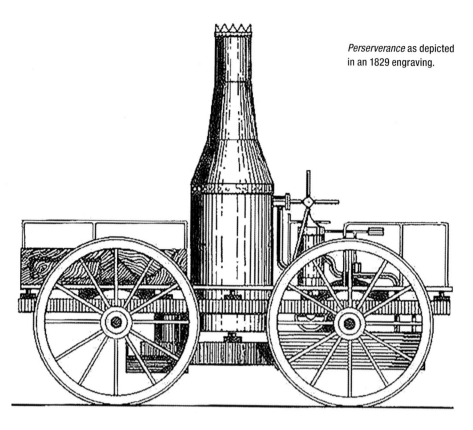

Perserverance as depicted in an 1829 engraving.

THE BIG DECIDER

Once Richard Trevithick's self-propelled locomotive had proved itself on the Penydarren Tramroad in 1804, a newcomer to railway history might be forgiven for thinking that from then on it would be a case of lighting the blue touch paper and watching the steam era mushroom overnight. In reality, it was anything but.

As we have seen, horse power remained king for the next quarter of a century. Yes, there were experimental locomotives built to Trevithick's concept in the industrial North East, but in that period, just 50 were built. Many still considered the steam locomotive little

more than a novelty. The Liverpool & Manchester Railway Company was divided between those who backed Stephenson and Locke, the pair both recommending the use of steam locomotives, and those that backed Stourbridge engineer and Trevithick collaborator John Urpeth Rastrick, who argued the case for stationary engines and cable haulage, and who, in 1829, built the *Stourbridge Lion*, the first successful steam locomotive to run in the United States.

The Stockton & Darlington used both stationary engines and horse traction as well as steam locomotives, and the Liverpool & Manchester Railway

A grandstand was erected to allow spectators to have a clear view of the proceedings at the Rainhill Trials of 1829.

The working replica of *Sans Pareil* inside the Locomotion museum at Shildon. ROBIN JONES

board sent observers to the Durham line in a bid to ascertain which form of motive power was the best. They reported back, but still the board could not decide. In the meantime, a host of weird and wonderful suggestions were made, ranging from inclined planes to a vacuum atmospheric system and a gas vacuum-powered engine.

On April 20, 1828, the directors decided to hold a series of trials in a bid to ascertain which direction would prevail for future plans. They offered a £500 prize for "a Locomotive Engine which shall be a decided improvement on those now in use" – and stipulated that the locomotives entered for the contest must be capable of covering 70 miles without breaking down – i.e. a return journey over the Liverpool & Manchester. The locomotives were to be restricted to a weight of 4½ tons on four wheels, and carried on springs to reduce potential track damage to the track. For the same reason, the boilers could not be too big. Locomotives entered were required to pull trains of only three times their weight.

Neither could the boiler be too big, in case its weight also led to track damage.

On August 31, 1829, the board announced the trials would be held over 1¾ double-tracked miles of the Liverpool & Manchester Railway. What became known as the Rainhill Trials was to become another landmark moment in world transport history.

George Stephenson decided to enter and, it is believed, started designing his locomotive for the contest in May that year. An 0-2-2 was to be named *Rocket*, and began its first trials on the Killingworth Railway on September 2, hitting 8mph up an incline and 12mph on the level.

The other entrants included *Novelty*, an 0-2-2 well tank, built in seven weeks in London by John Braithwaite to a design by the Swedish engineer John Ericsson; *Sans Pareil*, an 0-4-0 built by Timothy Hackworth as a private project in his spare time; and vertical-boilered four-wheeler *Perseverance*, built by

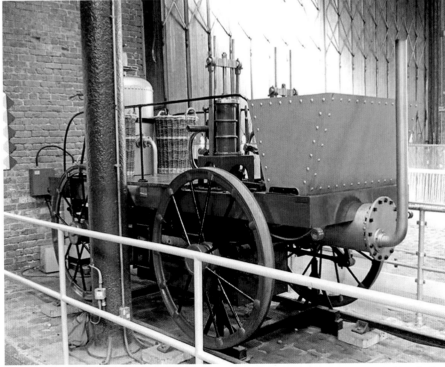

Rainhill entrant *Novelty*, an 0-2-2 well tank built by John Ericsson and John Braithwaite in 1829. A 'version' assembled in 1929 using many original parts is in the Museum of Science & Industry in Manchester. MOSI

The original *Sans Pareil* on display inside the Locomotion museum at Shildon. ASHLEY DACE*

Timothy Burstall, was based on a steam road coach design.

Former Liverpool & Manchester director and barrister Thomas Shaw, who argued that steam locomotives were dangerous, entered *Cycloped*, an 'engine' powered by two horses. Whenever its tethered horses tried to walk or trot, a platform of wooden planks attached to ropes supported by rollers caused two drums to revolve and move the four-wheeled open truck which comprised the body.

The trials began on October 6 and drew huge crowds, including leading engineers and scientists.

The first day saw *Rocket* hit 18mph while running light, whereas *Novelty* reached 30mph, while poor *Cycloped* hauled a short rake of wagons carrying about 50 people and reached 5mph, and took no further part.

On October 8, *Rocket* achieved a top speed of 29mph and an average of 16mph.

The next day, *Sans Pareil* steamed. It was claimed Stephenson was so

impressed by the more efficient blast it produced through its single exhaust pipe entering its chimney he had one immediately made in Warrington for *Rocket* and fitted it overnight – a move which saw the locomotive reach 30mph.

Sans Pareil and *Novelty* both sustained mechanical failures and were withdrawn, while *Perseverance* bowed out after managing just 6mph.

On the sixth and last day, *Rocket* hauled a carriage containing 25 passengers up an inclined plane at a speed of 20mph. It was declared the winner.

A pipe which had been smoked by Elizabethan explorer Sir Walter Raleigh just before his execution was presented to George Stephenson in honour of his achievement, while the railway not only bought *Rocket* but *Sans Pareil*, too.

THE GREATEST LEAP FORWARD

Rocket's place in history was not assured alone by the fact it won the Rainhill Trials.

Its key to immortality lay in the innovations that its designer – or maybe designers – introduced. Many historians believe far more of the work in building *Rocket* was undertaken by George's son Robert, the subject of Chapter 7.

Firstly, the use of a single pair of driving wheels, with a small carrying axle behind, was the most visible innovation. It made *Rocket* the first 0-2-2 and first single driver locomotive.

The use of single drivers gave several advantages. The weight of coupling rods was avoided and the second axle could be smaller and lightweight, as it only carried a small proportion of the weight. *Rocket* placed just over 2½ tons of its 4¼-ton total weight onto its driving wheels, a higher axle load than *Sans Pareil*, even though the rival 0-4-0 was heavier overall at five tons, and officially

disqualified by being over the 4½-ton limit.

Secondly, *Rocket* used a multi-tubular boiler design, whereas hitherto, locomotive boilers consisted of a single pipe surrounded by water. *Rocket's* 25 copper fire tubes carried the hot exhaust gas from the firebox, through the wet boiler to the blastpipe and chimney. The net result of this arrangement was a greatly increased surface contact area of hot pipe with boiler water over and above that which might be provided by a single large flue. Furthermore, radiant heating from the enlarged separate firebox helped deliver a further increase in steaming and hence boiler efficiency.

Rocket, however, was not the first multi-tubular boiler. French locomotive engineer Marc Seguin built two multi-tubular locomotives of his own design for the Saint-Étienne to Lyon railway before *Rocket* was outshopped from Forth Street Works in Newcastle.

Seguin had visited Stephenson to

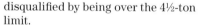

A contemporary drawing showing the entrants to the Rainhill Trials in action.

The National Railway Museum's working replica of *Rocket* heads a pair of reproduction Liverpool & Manchester Railway coaches along the Great Central Railway during the heritage line's 'Golden Oldies' gala of May 31, 2010. In 1979, the magnificent working replica was built by engineer Mike Satow and his Locomotion Enterprises for the Rocket 150 anniversary celebrations at Rainhill. It was displayed in Kensington Gardens, London, on the 150th anniversary of the Rainhill Trials. In 2009 it was completely rebuilt by Victorian locomotive restoration experts at Bill Parker's Flour Mill Colliery workshops at Bream in the Forest of Dean, not only with a new boiler, but also new frames, before returning to steam the following February. ROBIN JONES

observe *Locomotion* on the Stockton & Darlington Railway.

Thirdly, *Rocket* also used a blastpipe, feeding the exhaust steam from the cylinders into the base of the chimney in order to induce a partial vacuum and pull air through the fire.

George Stephenson had used blastpipes on his locomotives as early as 1814. The blastpipe excelled on the multi-tube boiler of *Rocket* whereas on earlier locomotives, with a single flue through the boiler, it had created so much suction it tended to rip the top off the fire and throw burning cinders out of the chimney, sending the fuel consumption soaring.

The fourth innovation comprised cylinders being closer to the horizontal. Most older designs had the cylinders positioned vertically, giving the engines an uneven swaying motion as they rode along the track. However, *Rocket* was modified so the cylinders were set close to horizontal, and established a

principle that influenced nearly all steam locomotive designs that followed.

Rocket's fifth innovation saw the pistons connected directly to the driving wheels, an arrangement adopted by subsequent steam locomotive designers.

Innovation number six was *Rocket's* firebox being separate from the boiler; it was double walled, with a water jacket

A contemporary sketch of *Rocket* by Samuel Smiles.

between them. Stephenson saw that the hottest part of the boiler, and therefore the most effective for evaporating water, was that surrounding the fire itself. This firebox was heated by radiant heat from the glowing coke, not just convection from the hot exhaust gas.

Rocket's first firebox was made from copper sheet and had a triangular shape when viewed from the side.

The throatplate and possibly the backhead were made of firebrick. When *Rocket* was rebuilt around 1831, this was replaced by a wrought iron backhead and throatplate, with a drum wrapper, probably copper.

This arrangement gave a larger internal volume and encouraged better combustion within the firebox, rather than inside the tubes.

In short, *Rocket* marked a watershed between the age of early steam locomotives that began with Trevithick and what was to follow in the sphere of steam locomotive evolution.

THE WORLD'S FIRST INTER-CITY RAILWAY

The Liverpool & Manchester Railway was not only the first in the world to link two major cities, and the first to offer a scheduled passenger service, but also the first to be built to 4ft 8½in gauge, what we now know as standard gauge.

When building the Stockton & Darlington Railway, George Stephenson carried over the 4f 8in gauge of his Hetton Railway. He chose this gauge to accommodate the gauge of hundreds of horse-drawn chaldron wagons that were already in use on horse-drawn tramways or mine rails in the North East.

Stephenson made a slight adjustment to the gauge for the Liverpool & Manchester Railway by adding the extra half inch for freer movement to reduce binding on curves. The creation of the Liverpool & Manchester involved four years of hard slog with several landmark engineering feats – the aforementioned crossing of Chat Moss, the building of the stupendous Sankey Viaduct, the hewing of thousands of tons of rock to create Olive Mount Cutting, and the boring of Edge Hill Tunnel to gain access to the heart of Liverpool.

Not only that, but the Stephensons had assembled a locomotive fleet for the line, including, of course, *Rocket*.

On June 14, 1830, a rake of seven wagons, carrying 80 stone blocks and two coaches, was hauled by Stephenson 0-2-2s Nos. 2 *Arrow* and 4 *Dart* from Liverpool to Manchester, at speeds of up to 25mph. The directors were impressed to say the least, and many lingering doubts about steam locomotives dispersed. They recorded their great appreciation "of the great skill and wearied energy displayed by their engineer, Mr George Stephenson".

Afterwards, directors made a series of weekly excursions along parts of the line. One, which ran on August 25, saw George Stephenson invite the famous actress Fanny Kemble, one of the passengers, to ride with him on the footplate. She afterwards wrote: "Now for a word or two about the master of all these marvels, with whom I am most horribly in love. He is a man from 50 to 55 years of age; his face is fine, though careworn, and bears an expression of deep thoughtfulness; his mode of explaining his ideas is peculiar and very original, striking, and forcible; and although his accent indicates strongly his north country birth, his language has not the slightest touch of vulgarity or coarseness. He has certainly turned my head." A portent of Isambard Brunel's "exertions with actresses" in Brighton, I mischievously wonder?

On September 15, 1830, the day of the official opening, huge crowds flocked to Liverpool to watch the trains depart, at Sankey Valley to watch them pass over the viaduct, and at Manchester to watch them arrive. Near Sankey Viaduct, a grandstand had been erected for 1000 people, and a ticket to enter cost 10s 6d, a fortune for most people at that time.

Steam traction then was still a novelty, just as public day trips by space shuttle to the moon and back would be in our time.

The roads approaching Liverpool had for several days beforehand been packed with visitors pouring into the port to attend the event, while others arrived by ship from Scotland and Ireland. Every hotel room and lodging-house in the city was full the night before. From 9am onwards the area around the station was filled with onlookers. It was clearly the biggest day of George Stephenson's life.

Tory Prime Minister Arthur Wellesley, the first of Duke of Wellington, agreed to open the railway, with three special carriages having been built. As he arrived, just before 10am, a band played See, the Conquering Hero Comes in praise of his victory over Napoleon at Waterloo. The duke's party boarded their carriage before a gun was then fired to mark the official opening of the railway. The carriages of the duke's train had their brakes released and were

An 1894 painting of *Northumbrian*, which hauled the Duke of Wellington's special train for the opening of the Liverpool & Manchester Railway, and which was the most advanced of the Stephenson 0-2-2s.

A painting of the first public service on the Liverpool & Manchester Railway.

Inter-city express! Liverpool & Manchester Railway 0-4-0 *Jupiter* hauls a rake of First Class carriages and a mail coach. The design of the carriages reflects the stagecoaches, which the railway network would make redundant.

allowed to roll down the incline under the force of gravity to be coupled to the waiting locomotive at the bottom.

Soldiers cleared onlookers from the tracks before a procession of trains left Crown Street station at 11am, all on time and without any technical problems.

Northumbrian, the last of *Rocket*-style 0-2-2s, hauled the duke's train, driven by George himself. It was the first locomotive to have the Stephenson-type firebox incorporated in the boiler, and having a smokebox the full diameter of the boiler it therefore boasted the first true 'locomotive' boiler, and was taking the development of the steam

locomotive on one step further than the Rainhill Trials winner. Much history good and bad was made on the day. Thirteen miles from Liverpool, a train hauled by *Phoenix* derailed and the train behind ran into it. It was the world's first collision between two passenger trains.

Worse, however, was to follow. The locomotives stopped at the midway point of Parkside station, 17 miles from Liverpool, to take on water, and the railway's officials told passengers to stay on board while this was taking place.

Tragically, this instruction was quickly forgotten when the duke's train arrived and around 50 of the guests aboard got

off. They included Liverpool MP William Huskisson, president of the Board of Trade and Treasurer of the Navy, who had done much to see the railway built, but had two years ago fallen out with the duke over the issue of parliamentary reform and resigned from the cabinet.

On the day, Huskisson was called to one side by William Holmes, the Tory Chief Whip, who told him the duke was in a particularly good mood owing to the cheering crowds which lined the route, and he might welcome an attempt at reconciliation, amid press speculation that he might be invited back into the Government.

George Stephenson's big moment of triumph: The Duke of Wellington's special train and other locomotives being readied for departure from Liverpool on September 15, 1830.

At the opposite end of the Edge Hill station area were the boilers of a stationary steam engine, which wound the rope hauling vehicles through the tunnels. They were each disguised as the base of a stylish Moorish arch, located within the Cavendish cutting. Sadly, this grand structure was demolished when the cutting was widened in the 1860s. However, Transport campaign group Liverpool Underground feels the city should act now in readiness for the 200th anniversary of the Liverpool-Manchester Railway on September 15, 2030 by rebuilding it. The group is calling on politicians and Merseytravel to make the idea a reality with the help of National Lottery Fund grant aid and crowdfunding.

Huskisson therefore approached the duke's carriage and shook his hand – but forgot the safety instructions, and took his eye off the ball, not noticing *Rocket* was approaching on the parallel track.

Rocket driver Joseph Locke could not slam on the locomotive's brakes because as an engineering prototype, it did not have any. So he put the engine into reverse gear, but it was too late.

Holmes clung to the side of the duke's carriage, but found himself pressed against it. Huskisson tried to climb inside, but he misjudged the distance and grabbed the handle of the carriage door…which swung open leaving him hanging directly in the path of the oncoming *Rocket*. The locomotive hit the door, and Huskisson fell onto the tracks in front of the oncoming train, suffering leg injuries that were to prove fatal.

Northumbrian detached from the special to take Huskisson to hospital, and thus formed the world's first ambulance train. Huskisson was taken to the vicarage at Eccles and placed in the care of the wife of the vicar,

the Reverend Thomas Blackburne, while George Stephenson drove *Northumbrian* on to Manchester with Lord Wilton and collected four surgeons, who returned to Eccles riding on the tender. Sadly, Huskisson died the same evening, becoming the first railway fatality, a death that was widely reported.

However, a large crowd had gathered in Manchester to see the trains arrive, and was beginning to become restless, and the duke was persuaded to continue with his trip to appease them.

On reaching the outskirts of Manchester, it was clear the crowd was hostile: the duke had become unpopular as Prime Minister, particularly in the industrial North West, for persistently blocking reforms. At the Liverpool Road terminus, an angrier crowd waved banners and flags in protest and pelted the train with vegetables. On the return trip, the train was bombarded with objects thrown as missiles as it passed through Rainhill, scene of *Rocket's* earlier success.

Huskisson's death was a cause of great mourning, yet had the effect of boosting the new railway's publicity.

The day after the official opening, the railway started a regular timetabled service and a total of 6104 passengers were carried in the first week.

The Liverpool & Manchester's phenomenal success sparked off the Railway Mania, in which schemes to build railway routes big and small mushroomed all over Britain for the best part of two decades. Horse traction was now firmly in the past: the steam railway was here to stay.

The success of this project led to both Stephensons being employed to engineers at several other and bigger railway projects. Accordingly, the 'Stephenson gauge' became widespread and dominant in Britain.

However, Robert was reported to have said that if he had had a second chance to choose a standard gauge, he would have chosen one wider than 4ft 8½in. "I would take a few inches more, but a very few," he was quoted as saying.

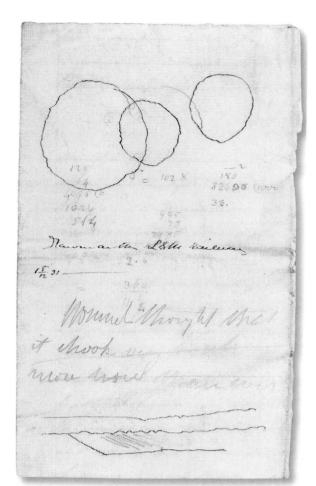

A CRITICAL EYE CAST...

While accolades poured into Merseyside by the day as the public were wowed by George Stephenson's futuristic means of travel between two cities, one passenger was not as impressed as he might have been, having found the ride bumpy.

On December 3, 1831, he wrote in his diary: "The time is not far off when we shall be able to take our coffee and write while going noiselessly and smoothly at 45 miles per hour… let me try."

His name? Isambard Kingdom Brunel.

Two years later, he would be given the chance to try – when he was appointed chief engineer for the Great Western Railway, the length of which he personally surveyed in its entirety in a bid to find the smoothest, flattest route.

Yes, he entered the fray many years after George Stephenson, but would emerge as one of his biggest rivals.

*These three pictures are reproduced by courtesy of the Brunel Institute – a collaboration of the ss Great Britain Trust and the University of Bristol.

ROCKET AFTER LIVERPOOL & MANCHESTER

Rocket remained in use on Liverpool & Manchester Railway after the accident, but was rarely used for anything other than internal engineering duties. In reality it was an engine built for winning a contest and for show rather than regular service, and innovations in steam technology were rapidly leaving it behind.

The Stephensons' more advanced *Planet* design was better suited to heavy loads, and *Rocket* became redundant. In 1834 it was used for experiments with new drive systems, after which it was stored. Two years later, in a much modified form, it was sold for £300 to the Brampton Railway, a mineral operation in Cumberland that had recently been converted to Stephenson's gauge. Used to haul coal until 1844, it was donated to the Patent Office Museum in London in 1862, now the Science Museum.

As stated in Chapter Two, in 2018 *Rocket* – of which several working and non-working replicas have been made over the past century – was loaned to Tyneside's Discovery Museum between June 22 and September 9, as a key exhibit in the Great Exhibition of the North.

During the 80 days *Rocket* was on display there, it was seen by more than 176,000 visitors. Discovery Museum and archives manager Carolyn Ball said: "It's been hugely popular. It's been one of the star attractions of Great Exhibition of the North."

On September 20, it was removed and taken by lorry to Manchester, to be displayed until April 28, 2019 at the Science & Industry Museum in Manchester, which includes the Liverpool Road terminus station *Rocket* served nearly two centuries ago.

In 2019, it is due to be moved to York, where it will become a permanent exhibit in the National Railway Museum.

SCIENCE MUSEUM

WEB TECHNOLOGY BROADCASTS HIDDEN SECRETS OF *ROCKET*

By Robin Jones

MODERN technology is unlocking the deepest secrets of Stephenson's *Rocket* to a worldwide audience for the first time – and you can build your own model with a 3D printer!

On the internet, the Science Museum Group has published a high-resolution 3D model of the 1829-built Rainhill Trials winner, enabling audiences across the globe to examine it in unprecedented detail.

Rocket secured its place in history after winning the 1829 trials for the Liverpool & Manchester Railway, reaching a top speed of 30mph. Manufactured earlier that year by Robert Stephenson & Company in Forth Street, Newcastle, *Rocket* brought together several efficiency and performance innovations, all of which are highlighted on the 3D model.

They included the multi-tubular boiler design and blastpipe, the use of a single pair of driving wheels, with a small carrying axle behind, making *Rocket* the first 0-2-2, and cylinders closer to the horizontal, all of which helped make it the fastest locomotive of its time. Its ground-breaking design became the basis for subsequent steam locomotive development over the next 150 years.

The 3D model of *Rocket* has been published on the Science Museum Group Collection website at: https://tinyurl.com/yd2twe4t

Audiences can move the 3.3-ton locomotive around with ease on screen, inspect underneath and explore the innovations.

The model can also be downloaded from Sketchfab (sketchfab.com/models) under a Creative Commons non-commercial licence, enabling users to 3D print their own model of *Rocket*.

Measuring more than 13ft in length, *Rocket* is the most complex and largest

The 1829 notebook of steam engineer John Rastrick, one of the judges of the Rainhill Trials, detailing *Rocket*. On loan from the National Railway Museum, it is displayed alongside *Rocket* in the Manchester museum. NRM

item from the Science Museum Group Collection to be 3D scanned

Created using 22 high resolution LIDAR scans and more than 2500 detailed photographs, the 3D model has been published on the Science Museum Group Collection website and on Sketchfab, the world's largest 3D content platform.

Working with Science Museum Group colleagues, a team from ScanLAB spent 11 hours recording every angle of *Rocket* to create the 3D model, using more than 200kg of camera, lighting and scanning equipment. Scanning and photography was particularly challenging because of *Rocket's* colour, glossy texture and complex shape, said a spokesman for the group.

After six weeks of processing the LIDAR data and 220GB of photography, a highly detailed point cloud was produced, containing spatial coordinates, colour and intensity values for a staggering 750 million points.

A further two weeks of processing was needed to produce several 3D models of *Rocket,* one of which – featuring 84,000 vertices – was published as *Rocket* went on public display at the Science & Industry Museum in Manchester, which includes the Liverpool Road station that the locomotive served nearly two centuries ago.

Chapter 4

BIG CHANCE, BIGGEST RAILWAY

When Isambard Kingdom Brunel rode on George Stephenson's Liverpool & Manchester Railway, experienced a bumpy ride, and wrote in his diary he could do better, fate had it he would not be kept waiting too long…

PEACE, law and order returned to Bristol when the riots ended with the passing of the Reform Act. A new-found confidence descended on both the country and the city, and finance became available for improvements to the Floating Harbour. Bristol's great waterfront had been built by canal engineer William Jessop between 1804-10. He dammed the River Avon at Cumberland Basin and near Temple Meads, and diverted it through a new channel on the south side of the city centre.

Until then, the enormous tidal range in the Severn estuary, which gave a 30ft difference between high and low tides (the reason for the mudflats being passed off as beaches at such places as Clevedon and Weston-super-Mare) saw ships berthed in Bristol faced with grounding on the muddy bottom of the river estuary – hardly an incentive to modern international trade.

The Floating Harbour brought new prosperity to the city, and the Committee for Bristol Docks – on which Nicholas Roch was a member – sought further improvements to Jessop's artificial waterway.

It was Roch, alongside his friend Isambard, who had enlisted as a special constable during the previous year's riots. In 1832, Roch brought in Isambard, who had already gained some experience of designing docks. Back in Bristol, which would prove to be Isambard's happy hunting ground, he advised on the installation of sluices and an underfall dam at Rownham for regulating water inflow and scouring silt. He would return periodically to the improvement of the city's docks.

In 1843, Isambard designed a steam-powered drag boat constructed in riveted iron plate. It had winches for warping itself across the harbour, scraping the floor and walls as it went – and it remained in use until 1961.

He also designed a new south entrance lock, which was completed in 1849, and which used the first wrought-iron buoyant gate.

Isambard's work in Bristol greatly raised his standing in the port, and as we shall see, opened the door for arguably his greatest triumphs.

Boosting Bristol's facilities to accept more and bigger trading vessels was a major step forward, but how do you handle the resulting large volume of imports and exports? The major rival port of Liverpool had a new futuristic form of transport already serving its hinterland and beyond – the Liverpool & Manchester Railway, by then a proven and renowned success story.

In 1832, two proposals for a London to Bristol railway were issued, but both of them failed to raise sufficient capital. However, it would be third time lucky, because that autumn four Bristol businessmen – Thomas Guppy, John and William Harford, and George Jones – sought to develop the idea and enlist the support of those with greater influence.

On January 21, 1833, a meeting was held between the Merchant Venturers, who had supported Isambard Brunel over the suspension bridge project, Bristol Corporation, the Bristol Dock Company, the Chamber of Commerce and the Bristol & Gloucestershire Rail Road Company, to investigate the feasibility of linking Bristol to London by rail.

Again, Roch turned to his old friend after being tasked with finding a suitable engineer for such a project. On February 21, 1833, Roch informed Isambard about the project, and he, along with several rivals, were invited to survey a route. The winner would be chosen on the basis of whichever project would be cheapest.

It might have been an easy task to

Ship shape and Bristol fashion: An etching published around 1850 showing the towers of St Stephen's Church, St Augustine the Less Church, Bristol Cathedral, and the historic harbour with 10 sailing ships and rowing boats before the channel was filled in from 1892-1938.

knock a nought off here and there, but Isambard was having none of it. When interviewed by the railway committee, Isambard laid the line 'on the line'.

He said he was prepared to survey only a route that was the best, not the most cost-effective. This put his reputation at stake – and he won.

The committee confirmed his appointment, and appointed local engineer W H Townsend as his

assistant, a man who had designed the horse-drawn, freight-only Bristol & Gloucestershire Railway, which ran from coal mines at Coalpit Heath to the River Avon at Cuckold's Mill.

Members ordered Isambard to survey the route to London within a month, and he set out on horseback for the purpose.

Very soon, far fewer people would ride from Bristol to London using equine transport.

GOD'S WONDERFUL RAILWAY: THE SEEDS ARE SOWN

Isambard's choice of route from Bristol was costed at around £2.8million.

The project received a formal launch at the Bristol Guildhall on July 30, 1833. A decision was taken to form a company to build the railway, drawing directors from both Bristol and London for a general board of management ,

Separate committees were formed in each city. On August 22, 1833, the first joint meeting of the London & Bristol Railroad was held at the offices of Gibbs & Sons, in Lime Street, in the City of London. However, the name changed by the time the share issue prospectus appeared, and global transport history was duly made.

It was to be called the Great Western Railway.

Worryingly, by October that year, only around 25% of the capital had been raised. Yet on September 7, Isambard was asked to begin work on the detailed survey, and set off again on horseback.

Parliamentary sanction would be the first major stumbling block if 50% of the capital had not been raised, and so on October 23, the directors announced two railways would be built: the first from London to Reading with a branch to Windsor, and the second from Bristol to

Bath. They would continue to raise funds in the hope of the lines being joined up at a later date.

In March 1834, the Great Western Railway Bill was passed in the House of Commons by 182 votes to 92, but had then to go to Committee stage. The committee, chaired by Lord Granville Somerset, met on April 16 – and then sat for 57 days to discuss the bill, as those raising objections had the right to be heard individually.

Might this hearing have been an early definition of NIMBYism (Not In My Back Yard)?

Objectors argued passengers would be "smothered in tunnels" and "necks would be broken", and that the water supply for Windsor Castle would be destroyed. A farmer voiced fears his cattle would die if they passed under a railway bridge. The provost of Eton College claimed the railway would be "dangerous to the morals of the pupils".

Isambard was cross-examined in the witness stand for 11 days, and after the committee approved the bill, it was returned to the Commons, only to rejected by the House of Lords on July 25, 1834 by 47 votes to 30. In the meantime, public support for the railway

had soared, and it was just a matter of time before victory would be assured.

In September 1834, the company issued a new prospectus for a complete 116-mile trunk railway running via Bath, Chippenham, Wootton Bassett, Swindon, Wantage, Reading, Maidenhead and Slough, longer than the shorter route between Bradford-on-Avon, Hungerford and Devizes, but offering access to Oxford, Cheltenham and the Gloucestershire wool trade, and the potential for an extension to the flourishing South Wales coalfield.

Sufficient capital was raised for a second bill to be presented to Parliament, and while the London & Southampton Railway objected because it could offer a shorter route to Bath, and the debate lasted 40 days, it received Royal Assent on August 31, 1835. A clause stipulated the route could not pass within three miles of the aforementioned Eton College.

Work began within a matter of weeks, and Isambard was all set to steal a march on his rival railway builders everywhere.

He would also spring a major surprise on both his directors and the wider embryonic railway world.

THE WIDER THE BETTER

The 1834 bill – thrown out by the House of Lords – included a clause which stipulated the new railway should be built to a gauge of 4ft 8½in; 'gauge' being the space between the rails.

That was the gauge to which George Stephenson had built the Liverpool & Manchester Railway, and which we have long since called standard gauge.

However, Isambard was having none of it. He contemptuously referred to Stephenson's railway as having been built to "horse-truck" gauge, because it could use rolling stock from industrial railways in mines, factories and quarries.

On September 15, 1835, Isambard recommended to the company directors that in respect to gauge, there should be "a deviation from the dimensions adopted in the railways hitherto constructed" – and quoted friction, resistance and wheel size to support a wider gauge.

Isambard argued there would be advantages in reducing the centre of gravity of rolling stock by mounting coach and wagon bodies between the wheels rather than above them. Also, a

A contemporary sketch showing the difference in size between Isambard Brunel's 7ft 0¼in gauge and George Stephenson's smaller 4ft 8½in.

wider gauge would offer bigger and more powerful locomotives and carriages and wagons with a greater capacity.

In short, Isambard's argument was that a broad gauge made possible a smoother, more stable and potentially faster service. He proposed a gauge of between 6ft 10in and 7ft.

His only precedent was that his father Marc had laid a 7ft-gauge track in Chatham Docks for transporting timber from a sawmill.

Instead of the conventional railway track of rails fixed on sleepers set in ballast, Brunel's broad gauge utilised heavy timbers laid under the track longitudinally, with cross ties for spacing every 15ft – just as was the case with the Chatham system.

Hired on a £2000-a-year salary, Isambard settled on 7ft gauge, adding an extra quarter inch for clearance purposes.

Isambard persuaded Lord Shaftesbury, chairman of committees in the House of Lords, to drop the gauge clause from the second Great Western Railway bill; it was drawn up, and had no mention of track gauge.

In those infant days of Britain's railway system, there was no 'standard' gauge, and new railways often went their own way, at least at the start, but converting to Stephenson gauge later.

England's Eastern Counties Railway was originally built to 5ft gauge, several new Scottish lines chose 5ft 6in, the Ulster Railway chose 6ft 2in, and the Dublin & Drogheda Railway selected 5ft 2in, later adding an inch, to which Irish main line railways became the norm. India, Pakistan, Sir Lanka, Bangladesh, Spain, Portugal, Argentina and Chile opted for 5ft 6ins, Brazil and parts of Australia went for 5ft 3in, while the former Soviet Union states, Finland and Outer Mongolia chose 5ft gauge. However, Stephenson gauge was adopted by most of Europe, the USA, Canada, Mexico, China, South Korea,

Broad gauge and mixed gauge track on Didcot Railway Centre's demonstration line. ROBIN JONES

Venezuela, Paraguay, Uruguay, and parts of Argentina, Brazil and Australia.

Isambard saw the downside of adopting an 'odd' gauge from the start, knowing his Great Western Railway could never run 'through' trains onto a standard gauge system. However, he did not set out to build his railway to a new national 'norm' but just wanted the best, with no more bumpy rides between cities!

His choice of gauge created an initial problem regarding the proposed London terminus.

As originally planned, the GWR would share Euston station with the London & Birmingham Railway – which would be built to Stephenson gauge. There followed a dispute between the two companies over land rights, which led to the GWR deciding to build a terminus of its own in a village called Paddington, on the westernmost edge of London.

The original GWR Paddington station, sketched on the day it opened, was very much a minimalist affair at what was then a rural village to the west of the metropolis.

WESTWARD BOUND

The year 1836 marked two major milestones for Isambard. Firstly, on July 5, at Kensington, he married Mary Horsley. Her brother was accomplished painter John Horsley, a member of the Royal Academy, who was later to paint his portrait.

Secondly, work began on building the Great Western Railway.

The first contract for the construction of the line had been let in September 1835 for the building of a stupendous 891ft-long viaduct at Hanwell across the River Brent in London, comprising eight brick arches with a span of 70ft, the highest being 65ft.

It was named after Lord Wharncliffe, who had helped the GWR bill through the Lords; it still carries his coat of arms today.

As with his original Clifton suspension bridge design, Isambard opted for an Egyptian style for the structure, mirroring the contemporary trend towards neo-classical architecture.

As an aside, Isambard was quick to see the possible advantages of the early electric telegraph system for use in running the railway. In 1838 he persuaded Sir Charles Wheatstone and William Fothergill Cooke to install their five-needle telegraph system between Paddington station and West Drayton, and to carry out experiments. Accordingly, this

One of the architectural treasures of Ealing is Wharncliffe Viaduct, the first major engineering project completed by Isambard Kingdom Brunel. It can be found to the west of Hanwell station. MARK HILLARY*

The Wharncliffe coat of arms as it appears on the south side of Wharncliffe Viaduct. PG CHAMPION*

BELOW: Original drawings for Brunel's nature-defying, elliptical double-span Maidenhead bridge. NETWORK RAIL

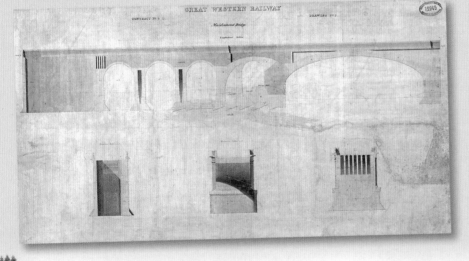

viaduct ended up carrying the world's first commercial electrical telegraph – on April 9, 1839.

Yet the world and its bridge builders had seen nothing yet.

Gargantuan as it was, Hanwell Viaduct would never match the architectural splendours of the semi-elliptical, twin-span bridge taking the main line across the Thames at Maidenhead.

It would become part and parcel of the package that bestowed Isambard with legendary status, and one of his finest works of all.

He needed to use the River Thames at a point where it was 100ft wide and was also a navigable waterway, which ruled out building multiple supports from the river bed, or placing any obstruction in it. The river had to be left clear for the passage of barges (which, ironically, would soon be rendered extinct by the railway in any case).

Isambard could have raised the height of his railway bridge, but that would have broken the 1-in-1320 smooth ruling gradient between London and Didcot.

Here, Isambard stretched the laws of physics to its known limits, and maybe beyond. His brick bridge had just one support in the middle, with his critics claiming the bridge, the largest brick feature on the London to Bristol line, would never stand up.

It is still there today and in active railway service.

Built in 1838 and designed by Isambard Kingdom Brunel, the two arches of Maidenhead bridge over the River Thames were, when built, the flattest and widest bridge arches in the world. Critics said they would collapse, but as of 2018 they are still standing! ANDREW BOWDEN*

WHERE WAS ISAMBARD'S 'ROCKET'?

History records that *Rocket* paved the way for the phenomenal success of the Liverpool & Manchester Railway, and indeed, set in stone the principle that steam locomotives were the future of transport technology, and not just a novelty in a world dominated by horse-drawn traction.

Isambard's Great Western Railway needed not only an equivalent but something much better, especially taking the wider gauge into account.

Brunel had already shown himself to be a brilliant structural engineer, as with Maidenhead Bridge. However, when it came to steam locomotives, he was trailing badly behind the Stephensons, and knew he had to do much more to make his railway work.

As the first length of the GWR was under construction, he ordered an assortment of 19 locomotives from various manufacturers who he had provided with basic specifications to follow and left them to design the rest. The end results were at best patchy in performance. And indeed, after the initial length to Taplow had opened, it became clear only six of the them were capable of running.

One of the failures had been built to an absurd design with a 10ft driving wheel on a 2-2-2 leading truck, and with its boiler mounted on a chassis trailing behind.

A saving grace was none other than Robert Stephenson, who supplied a 2-2-2- locomotive, *North Star*, which had been built for the 5ft 6in-gauge New Orleans Railway before the order had been cancelled.

Regauged to 7ft 0¼in, *North Star* arrived at Maidenhead by barge at the end of November 1837 and waited there until tracklaying reached that

J M W Turner's Rain, Steam and Speed depicts an early broad gauge train, possibly near Maidenhead Bridge.

point in May 1838. *North Star* proved so successful that a sister locomotive, *Morning Star*, was ordered, and another 10 were bought.

However, just as Isambard had been given his big chance at such an early age, it was his turn to follow likewise, when a 20-year-old named Daniel Gooch wrote to him inquiring about the position of locomotive engineer on the GWR.

Gooch was no idle daydreamer or fantasist. As a teenager he had worked at Robert Stephenson's Vulcan Foundry in Newton-le-Willows and helped his brother, T L Gooch, survey the London & Birmingham and Manchester & Leeds railways.

Isambard interviewed him and was so impressed he took him on at £300

GWR locomotive engineer Daniel Gooch with a model 2-2-2, which he commissioned from a London craftsman in 1840.

The original station at Maidenhead, accessed once the bridge over the Thames had been built.

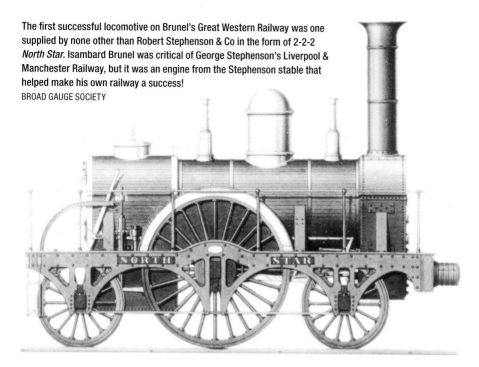

The first successful locomotive on Brunel's Great Western Railway was one supplied by none other than Robert Stephenson & Co in the form of 2-2-2 *North Star*. Isambard Brunel was critical of George Stephenson's Liverpool & Manchester Railway, but it was an engine from the Stephenson stable that helped make his own railway a success! BROAD GAUGE SOCIETY

a year. He never had cause to regret his decision.

Gooch was appalled at the sight of some of those early locomotives ordered by Isambard.

While the first section of the line was being completed, Gooch set up a basic locomotive-building operation for the company and produced workable designs for its future.

The London to 'Maidenhead' section (in reality only to Taplow, a mile short of the town) opened to paying passengers on June 4, 1838, although a directors' special had operated five days before behind *North Star*.

The following year, passenger services were extended over Maidenhead Bridge to Twyford, and the GWR board ordered Gooch to design and buy locomotives capable of handling this longer run.

He modified the 'Stars' by introducing the large haystack-style firebox so typical of broad gauge gauge engines, along with outside sandwich frames, a domeless boiler covered in wooden planks, and inside cylinders.

Fire Fly, the first of 62 hugely successful 2-2-2s of the Firefly class, was delivered, quickly sending the locomotives ordered by Brunel to the scrapheap. It was the start of a world-changing partnership between Isambard and Gooch, the civil engineering genius and the new master of steam technology.

The non-working replica of *North Star* was constructed for the GWR's 1923 Cavalcade, and is now housed at the STEAM – Museum of the Great Western Railway in part of Swindon Works. It made use of some of the parts of the original *North Star*, which was controversially scrapped in 1906, but is not capable of being steamed. Although it was featured in the railway's centenary film in 1935, it was pushed by another locomotive. ROBIN JONES

MAINTAINING PANCAKE LEVEL!

A view of the deepest part of Sonning Cutting taken from the bridge in Warren Road in early morning sunshine as a High Speed Train passes on August 16, 2007. The route has since been electrified. ANDREW SMITH*

The Paddington to Swindon section has often been nicknamed 'Brunel's billiard table' because of its gentle ruling gradient of 1-in-1320, designed to eradicate the bumpy rides he experienced on that Liverpool & Manchester Railway trip.

After Maidenhead Bridge, the next big physical obstacle to building a line with such a nearly-flat profile westwards was a hill at Holme Park, next to the village of Sonning, east of Reading, which blocked the way.

Isambard drew up plans for a mile-long tunnel, but GWR directors feared passengers would not want to spend so long in the dark, and then landowners agreed to allow the proposed tunnel to be opened out into a cutting.

The colossal Sonning Cutting, one of the biggest excavations of the early railway age, nearly two miles long and up to 60ft deep, took a team of 1200 navvies, aided by 200 horses, to dig it out during the summer of 1838.

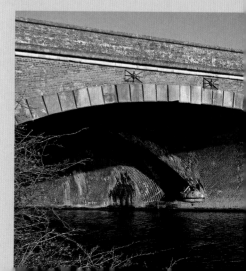

The cutting was produced by hand, using spades, with no machinery. Wheelbarrows and horse-drawn carts were used to remove the spoil. It took two years to complete and several people were killed in the process.

Because of a harsh winter, it wasn't until the end of 1839 the cutting was completed, along with a brick three-arch bridge to carry the main London to Reading road across it. There was also a smaller timber bridge that many have conjectured was the blueprint for the great trestle viaducts Isambard would build in Devon and Cornwall in the years ahead.

Laying broad gauge track took longer than a conventional railway with sleepers, and so the completion of the GWR exceeded the original completion date. The 30ft 'baulks' – laid between each cross-member or 'transom' at 15ft intervals and packed with ballast to form a firm foundation for the base – required far more labour and raw materials, not least of all the need to treat the pine to prevent rot. Here was one reason why this system of laying track was not adopted elsewhere in Britain.

On March 14, 1840, *Fire Fly* hauled a directors' train from Paddington to Reading and public services began on March 30.

The section from Reading to Steventon, on the Oxford turnpike road, opened on June 1, 1840, serving a coach connection to the city 10 miles away. It was superseded by a station at Didcot four years later. On July 20, 1840, rail services extended to Faringdon Road, 63½ miles from Paddington, later renamed Challow. On December 17, 1840, services were extended to Hay Lane, later officially named Wootton Bassett Road. On this date the GWR issued its first proper passenger timetable.

ABOVE: Everyday travellers on the broad gauge in the mid-19th century: Another cameo scene re-created by the aforementioned Ragged Victorians living history group at Didcot Railway Centre on October 14, 2018. FRANK DUMBLETON

BELOW: A Brunel broad gauge-era trackwork gang, re-created in a Ragged Victorians photographic event held at Didcot Railway Centre on October 14, 2018, organised by Neil Cave of Timeline Events. The Ragged Victorians - The Great Unwashed is an award-winning living history group, re-enacting the lower classes of Victorian England, c1851. FRANK DUMBLETON

Moulsford Viaduct still takes the Great Western main line over the River Thames, near Cholsey. ROBIN JONES

HUB OF AN ENGINEERING EMPIRE

Three miles back up the line from Wootton Bassett Road lay a sleepy market town called Swindon, on the North Wilts Canal. Thanks to Isambard and his locomotive superintendent, it would be quiet no longer.

Swindon had already been chosen as the junction for the broad gauge Cheltenham & Great Western Union Railway, an independent line worked by the GWR, which opened on May 13, 1841.

Swindon station was opened on July 17, 1842. It was built by contractors J & C Rigby, at their expense, in return for the right to operate the refreshment rooms on the ground floor and a hotel on the upper ones.

This company obtained an agreement from the GWR for all trains to stop there for 10 minutes so refreshments could be bought, while locomotives were changed. They comprised the first recorded railway refreshment rooms, and were divided according to class.

A popular myth has it Brunel and Gooch were surveying a vale north of Swindon Hill when they chose the town for the site of the GWR's central workshops. The story runs Brunel either threw a stone or dropped a picnic sandwich and declared that spot to be the new location of the works.

In reality, the selection of that particular site most likely had more to do with the location of the canal, which would bring in supplies of coal from the Somerset mines for the locomotives as well as basic building materials.

Also, because the terrain west of Swindon became more hilly than 'Brunel's billiard table' from there to Paddington, engines had to be changed because a different type of locomotive would be needed for the gradients.

GWR directors gave the go-ahead to Gooch's plans for Swindon Works in February 1841. Work began

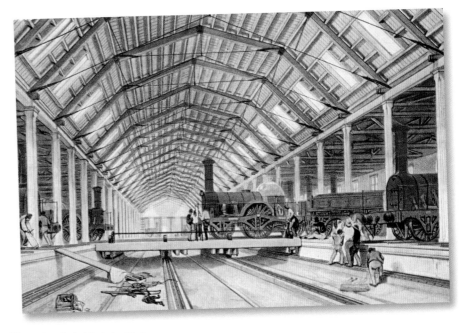

The engine shed at Swindon Works as depicted by J C Bourne in its early years, and later coloured.

immediately, with many of the buildings constructed with stone obtained during the excavation of Box Tunnel, further to the west.

By January 1843, Swindon Works already employed 400 men, including 72 highly skilled engineers.

Determined to avoid the squalid back-to-back houses associated with the new wave of industrial boom towns, the GWR built Swindon Railway Village, a model settlement of terraced houses, which offered far better accommodation for the average labourer or factory worker of the day.

The work's first locomotive, a classic broad gauge 2-2-2 named *Great Western*, emerged in April 1846, and was to become the forerunner of Gooch's hugely successful Iron Duke class.

Jumping a track or two here, in 1855

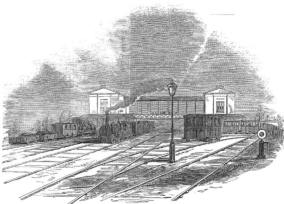

The original Swindon station.

production of standard gauge engines began as the GWR empire absorbed more and more 4ft 8½in-gauge lines. In 1861, a mill to produce rails was set up inside the expanding works, and in June 1868 a new carriage and wagon works was opened. By then, sleepy Swindon had become a metropolis in miniature.

Building the great incline at Wootton Bassett, as sketched by J C Bourne.

Isambard Brunel's stylish cutting through Bath's Sydney Gardens, as seen in 2006. ROBIN JONES

BOXING CLEVER TO BRISTOL…AND BEYOND

Work on building the section west of Swindon began in 1837, and from Wootton Bassett, where a huge incline was created, major earthworks were required. The line from here to Bristol ran over the hilly southern Cotswolds, and presented the young railway builder with his biggest challenge so far – exacerbated by constant rain during the wet winter of 1839, causing landslips at many of the embankments built from the spoil, which had been excavated from the cuttings.

To the south of Chippenham station stands the 90-yard Grade II-listed Cotswold stone Chippenham Viaduct, also known as the Western Arches, and which looks the same as it did when built, despite its being widened in the early 20th century.

Leaving the town, the railway runs along an embankment for two miles, and then through a deep cutting leading to the biggest obstacle on the entire line, an outlier of the Cotswolds known as

The striking neo-classical western portal of Box Tunnel, as drawn by J C Bourne. BRUNEL 200

Brunel's bridge over the Bristol Avon, to the west of Bath station, was replaced by a steel bridge in the 1890s.

ABOVE RIGHT: J C Bourne's illustration of the interior of Box Tunnel. Some passengers preferred to get out at one end, and take a road coach to the other end so they could continue their journey by train.

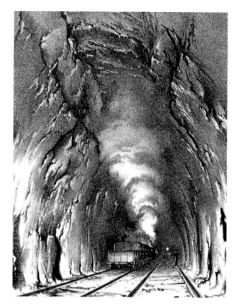

Bath station as built by Brunel and sketched by J C Bourne.

Isambard Brunel's broad gauge railway offered many advantages, but just as with other locomotive types of the day, its first engines offered not even basic protection to the elements for the drivers and firemen. Lacking cabs, they had to face the onslaught of wind, rain and snow, while not only setting record-breaking speeds, but doing their best to keep to the timetable.

Box Hill, between Corsham and Box.

Here stood the biggest test of all for Isambard. This was his Chat Moss moment, and he did not baulk at the prospect.

He drew up plans for a two-mile tunnel through the hill, but many critics were aghast. There was a ruling 1-in-100 gradient, and one Member of Parliament feared if the brakes failed, a train could run out of control through the pitch black, accelerating up to speeds of 120mph and suffocate all those on board in the process.

Another MP told the Commons if the tunnel was built, nobody would be brave enough to enter it. Undeterred, Isambard and his resident engineer William Glennie set about excavating the tunnel in September 1836; it would take five years to build.

Up to 1200 navvies toiled round the clock on the tunnel scheme, rising to 4000 in the final few months, with a team of 100 horses to take away the 247,000 cubic yards of spoil which had been excavated.

A ton each of gunpowder and candles was used each week, and echoing the Thames Tunnel, there were delays because of flooding. It has been said the gruelling conditions claimed the lives of up to 100 navvies, with many more injured or maimed.

In early spring 1841, the two ends of the tunnel met and daylight shone through. The fact the side walls lined up within an inch and a half were testament to Isambard's calculations. He spared no expense in adding his distinctive grandiose style, finishing the portals in Bath stone to a classical style.

On June 30, 1841, one of the twin tracks could be used by trains. It was reported a few passengers left the train before the tunnel and rejoined it on the other side.

Not only did the two ends of the tunnel line up, but the triumph that was Box – the longest tunnel on any railway in Britain at 9636ft – marked the completion of the entire route, as the

The castellated western portion of Twerton Tunnel again highlights Isambard Brunel's insistence of neo-classical designs for his railway wherever possible, as opposed to the more functional and workaday architectural designs of his rivals elsewhere. ROBIN JONES

Isambard Brunel's original Bristol Temple Meads terminus for the GWR line from London. ROBIN JONES

line from Bristol eastwards had by then been built up to that point.

In Bath, there was another major hurdle to cross – the first purpose-built route between London and the Roman city, in the form of the Kennet & Avon Canal.

A section of the canal at Sydney Gardens, a popular Bath pleasure park, needed to be diverted. Isambard yet again tore up the rule book and came up with a 27ft-high retaining wall, which was five feet thick in places, in order to create a barrier between his railway cutting and the canal. In another stylish touch, he provided a stone and an ornamental cast-iron bridge to link the two parts of the park, which had been bisected by both railway and canal, and added a skewed stone bridge to carry Sydney Road.

The railway passed through Regency Bath mostly on embankments and viaducts, with Isambard working overtime to avoid needless destruction to the fabric of the city.

He followed the canal and Bristol Avon as closely and possible, crossing the river twice, either side of Bath station, with an acutely skewed stone bridge on the Bristol side. The splendid two-storey frontage of Bath Spa station was designed by Brunel to a Jacobean style.

Bath's 18th-century magnificence was left intact, while the south side of the city became dominated by railway viaducts and embankments.

Two tunnels took the line through the Carrs Woodland hillside in Twerton; the bigger of them, Twerton Long Tunnel, has a castellated western portal, again designed to give passengers a sense of grandeur. Altogether, there were six tunnels between Bath and Bristol, although none as gargantuan as the one at Box, and most of them had classical portals.

Approaching the terminus, the railway crossed a mile of arches, a 100ft span across the Bristol Avon, and then a larger one to take it over the Floating Harbour.

GATEWAY TO THE WORLD

Work on building Bristol Temple Meads station, the western terminus, started in 1839 and took two years. Isambard was banned from building his station within the medieval walls of the city, so Temple Meads was the next best site. The name Temple Meads comes from the nearby Temple Church, built by the Knights Templar, the great medieval monastic order of crusading warriors.

Isambard constructed his station on a viaduct to raise it above the level of the Floating Harbour, and on the same scale as a cathedral. Temple Meads, not Paddington, was the first and foremost of the GWR termini, and it would be another 14 years before the company bestowed London with a structure of the same size and prominence. Indeed, the Bristol Committee had been dismayed by the near-minimalist original Paddington terminus, and insisted Isambard provided something that was far more grandiose – just what the engineer wanted to hear.

When completed, the timber and iron roof of the Temple Meads passenger shed formed the widest single span of the day, supported by 44 massive brick flattened arches, with a 74ft single-span wooden hammer beam roof, a copy of Westminster Hall, covering the 220ft-long train shed and its five tracks.

In the years since the GWR received its enabling Act and before it linked London to Bristol, Isambard had also been busy on another major railway project – the Bristol & Exeter Railway.

The merchants of Bristol wanted to see a railway built to Exeter, an important commercial centre and a port on the English Channel, one which afforded easier shipping connections to continental Europe. They promoted the Bristol and Exeter Railway, issued a prospectus on October 1, 1835, and appointed Isambard as engineer.

Its bill had an easy passage and was enacted on May 19, 1836. The Act

The Bristol & Exeter Railway's headquarters building still survives alongside Bristol Temple Meads station. ROBIN JONES

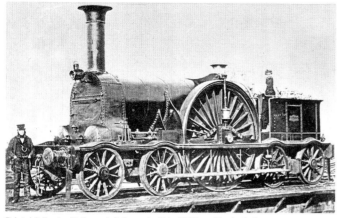

Bristol & Exeter Railway 4-2-2 was built in 1844, and typical of express passenger locomotives on the day, had a 9ft driving wheel. It lasted in service until 1870.

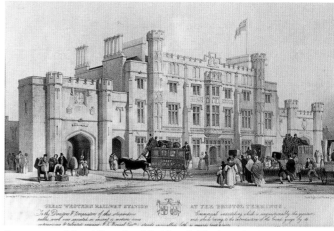

Passengers arriving at Brunel's original Temple Meads station by road coach.

did not specify the gauge of the track, and it was in March 1839 the company decided to go for Brunel's 7ft 0¼in broad gauge rather than Stephenson gauge, having seen how well the GWR was working. Train services from Bristol to Bath began on August 31, 1840, 10 months before the entire line to Paddington was completed on June 30, 1841.

However, shortly before, on June 14, the Bristol & Exeter Railway had opened as far south as Bridgwater, and at first it used the GWR's Bristol station. On July 8, 1844, the Bristol & Gloucester Railway, which had been initially built to broad gauge, entered Temple Meads, and also used the GWR platforms. Taken over by the Midland Railway on July 1, 1845, on May 29, 1854, a third rail

was laid on the Bristol to Gloucester line to create mixed gauge, so it could accommodate both Brunel broad gauge and Stephenson standard gauge trains.

That year, the Bristol & Exeter opened its own temporary station in 1845, at right angles to the GWR structure, following it up with a permanent one, designed by Samuel Fripp in Jacobean style in 1854.

As well as the Bristol & Exeter and Bristol & Gloucester, Brunel also designed the Bristol and South Wales Union Railway, which was completed on August 25, 1863, four years after his death. It also ran into Temple Meads.

As traffic levels rose, Temple Meads became outmoded, but it was not until 1865 that an Act of Parliament was obtained to rebuild it. Containing seven

platforms, it opened on January 1, 1878.

The Bristol & Exeter Railway opened to Exeter St David's station on May 1, 1844, giving, together with the GWR, a 194-mile Brunel broad gauge line from London.

On July 4, 1844 the South Devon Railway obtained its Act of Parliament, and would eventually extend the broad gauge from Exeter to Plymouth. Again, Isambard was appointed engineer, as he would also be on the Cornwall Railway from Plymouth to Truro, which issued its prospectus in 1844. However, as we will see in Chapter 6, Isambard may have exceeded his limits when engineering the South Devon Railway, both in terms of motive power, and also the choice of coastal route, an issue which still besets travellers today.

J C Bourne's depiction of the interior of the original Bristol Temple Meads station.

SPANNING THE ATLANTIC

For Isambard Brunel, the name Great Western Railway meant exactly 'what it said on the tin'. Not just running trains from London to Bristol, and beyond to Devon and Cornwall, he saw his line as doing what no other could do – running to the very far west – across the Atlantic to the United States.

While he was busy building the GWR and planning or constructing associated broad gauge lines, workhorse Isambard was designing no less than the world's first transatlantic liners.

Shipping was the last major area to benefit from the massive strides in transport technology, which had been spawned by the Industrial Revolution, and in Isambard's day was still sail power, with the industry having yet to embrace steam technology.

William Symington was the waterborne equivalent of Richard Trevithick. Born in Leadhills, Lanarkshire, in 1764, the son of a mechanic at local lead mines, he became a pioneer in steam mining technology. Having established a proven track record, he was asked by Patrick Miller, banker and shareholder in Carron Company, Scotland's premier engineering firm, to install a steam engine inside a pleasure boat for small-scale trials.

In 1812, Henry Bell launched the *Comet* on the Clyde. It was the first steam-operated commercial ferry, and was followed two years later by the steamboat *Regent*, running between London and Margate – and designed by none other than Marc Brunel.

The first cross-channel steamship was the 112-ton *Hibernia*, which made it from Holyhead to Dublin in seven hours in 1816. The first oceanic crossing by a steamship was made in 1819 by the *PS Savannah*, built by Francis Fickett, of Corlears Hook, New York, but for the most part, the ship relied on its sails rather than its steam engine.

However, until 1835, steamships were still considered suitable only for short runs in comparatively shallow waters, not having the capacity to carry and burn sufficient coal for anything like a transatlantic voyage. Marc Brunel was among those who believed the consumption of coal by a steam engine would increase in proportion with the size of a ship, and if these vessels could not cross an ocean, it followed neither could a much larger one.

It needed a genius to rewrite such accepted thinking, and one was found in Isambard Brunel. He realised the energy needed to drive a ship, whether by sail or steam, did not depend on the vessel's weight, but on the weight of the water that it has to shift.

He worked out the bigger the vessel, the better the crucial energy-to-weight equation.

Permanently housed in its dock alongside Bristol's Floating Harbour is the *ss Great Britain*, which was meticulously restored after being repatriated from the Falkland Islands. It is one of Isambard Kingdom Brunel's greatest achievements, being a major tourist attraction and source of pride for the whole country.
ROBIN JONES

Isambard was said to have early on suggested adding a steamboat to be called the *Great Western*, after the company, so his railway would in effect take passengers all the way to New York.

Director Thomas Guppy persuaded three other board members – Robert Scot, Robert Bright and Thomas Pycroft – to set up a committee to look into the possibility, and naval captain Christopher Claxton, who Brunel had met while working on the city docks, gained access to official drawings of Admiralty vessels currently under construction.

A low-key prospectus called for the company to build not one but two 1200-ton steamships with 400hp engines, with many local people buying shares in the scheme, along with Isambard himself.

A new prospectus was issued before the first meeting of a new Great Western Steamship Company on March 3, 1836, giving further details of the proposed ships, at the estimated cost of £35,000 each. Five of the directors were also board members of the GWR.

Isambard recruited Bristol shipbuilder William Patterson, and it was inside his yard at Wapping in the

Designed by Isambard Brunel and launched in Bristol in 1837, the *Great Western* established the advantage of steam over sail for transatlantic travel, becoming the model for successive Atlantic paddle steamers.

The launch of *ss Great Britain* in 1843, as depicted in a print by John Walter.

Floating Harbour that the keel of the first ship was laid in June. At 205ft, it was the longest to have been laid in Britain.

Crowds gathered on August 28, 1836 to watch the stern post of the great wooden ship raised and the stern frame positioned. Lambeth manufacturer Maudslay, Son & Field, which had vast experience in building marine engines, and had worked many times for Marc Brunel, was selected to supply the pair for the ship. The engines, which had massive cylinders with a 73½in diameter and a stroke of 7ft, were to drive twin paddle wheels 28ft in diameter

The great day came on July 19, 1837, when more than 50,000 onlookers crowded into Bristol's docks to watch the ship being launched, and named the *Great Western* by Mrs Miles, the wife of one of the steamship company's directors.

On August 18, the *Great Western* was towed down the Avon estuary by the steam tug *Lion*, and, accompanied by the steam packet *Benledi*, used

a four-masted schooner rig to travel to London around the south coast of England as a sailing ship. In East India Dock, at Blackwall, much of the machinery was fitted by Maudslay over six months, and four days of engine trials saw the *Great Western* manage an average speed of 11 knots comfortably.

Isambard Brunel had again been proved right, but North Atlantic shipping companies in both London and Liverpool had also decided they wanted a piece of the action, and set about converting ships to compete with his steamship.

The British & American Steam Navigation Company hired the 703-ton *Sirius* in an attempt to make the first scheduled steamship crossing to the USA. In a bid to beat the *Great Western*, the Sirius set out with 22 passengers on board in March 1838, while the engines on Brunel's ship were still being tested.

The *Great Western* set out from Bristol on April 7, with just seven passengers – several having cancelled their bookings because of rumours doubting the ship's ability. It arrived at

New York on April 23, having made the crossing in just 17 days, but the *Sirius* was already moored there having run aground after exhausting its coal supply.

Enthralled by the race between the two ships, the Americans queued to board the *Great Western* and the captain was forced to issue tickets in order to control the numbers. On the return journey, the *Great Western* took 14 days to reach Britain, compared to the 18 taken by her rival, and showed that unlike its competitor, it could cross the Atlantic with passengers and cargo and still be left with coal to spare.

The *Great Western* was an immediate commercial success, making 67 crossings in eight years and silencing her critics for good. However, she could not fit through the lock gates leading into the Floating Harbour, and the harbour authorities refused to sanction wider gates to allow bigger ships to pass.

Isambard and his committee then planned a second and far bigger ship, but this time drawing on iron-hull technology dating back to 1787, when a 70ft-long canal barge was aptly built by John 'Iron Mad' Wilkinson.

Medium-sized, ocean-going, iron-hulled ships were built in Britain in the 1820s, and had the advantage of being 30% lighter than their wooden counterparts, while offering thinner sides and therefore more hull space, but they were far smaller than the vessels envisaged by Isambard.

He was inspired by the sight of the world's first propeller-driven ship – Francis Pettit Smith's *Archimedes* – and when it arrived in the Floating Harbour in May 1840, Brunel decided he wanted some of that technology. Realising a fully immersed propeller would be far more efficient than paddle wheels, in December 1840 he insisted the new ship should be driven exclusively by one.

The ship was launched on July 19, 1843, exactly six years after that of the paddle steamer *Great Western*. Royal Consort Prince Albert arrived from

A wax effigy of Isambard Brunel inside the *ss Great Britain*. ROBIN JONES

A 'glass sea' surrounds the waterline of the ship, acting as an airtight chamber protecting its lower hull. Visitors can descend beneath the glass and inspect the hull and its key component, the propeller. ROBIN JONES.

RIGHT: On the deck of the *ss Great Britain*, which made her comeback voyage following repairs in May 1852, afterwards working the route to Australia for 24 years. In 1876 she was bought by Antony Gibbs & Sons Co for use as a transatlantic cargo sailing ship, with her engines removed during the conversion, in a classic case of backwards technology. After difficulties rounding Cape Horn in April 1886, during which two masts were lost and severe leaks sprung, the stricken ship was sold to the Falkland Islands Company as a store ship for coal and wood, and in 1937 it was beached at Sparrow Cove, with holes knocked in her stern so she would never float again. However, a scheme to rescue this Brunel masterpiece led to her being refloated with the aid of a pontoon and on April 24, 1970, *ss Great Britain* was towed behind the salvage tug *Varius II* 7000 miles back to Britain. On July 5, thousands of spectators again lined the banks of the Avon estuary as the ship, now afloat again, was towed upstream to Bristol docks, and a fortnight later, a spring tide allowed her to be eased into the Great Western dry dock off the Floating Harbour. The meticulous restoration of the *ss Great Britain* took 35 years to complete, and she will now stay moored in the dry dock forever, as a lasting monument to the man who designed it. ROBIN JONES

London via the GWR on a special train driven by Daniel Gooch, and smashed a bottle of champagne on the bows, naming the ship the *ss Great Britain*. With a displacement of 3675 tons, compared to 2300 for the *Great Western*, it was the biggest ship in the world.

Following trials and fitting out, its first Atlantic crossing was made from Liverpool on July 26, 1845, arriving in New York just 15 days later, at an average speed of more than nine knots. Her second trip to the USA resulted in several incidents of propeller damage and it returned to Liverpool under sail power only, but still in just 20 days.

Its third voyage to New York, on May 29, 1846, saw the *ss Great Britain* make the crossing in just 13 days, at an average speed of 13 knots.

The GWR did not run regular services to New York as Isambard had hoped, but his application and enhancement of steam technology in a marine environment had succeeded in shrinking the globe. Just as the Stephensons pointed the way ahead through *Rocket* for the future of the steam railway locomotive, Isambard Brunel did the same for the ocean liner.

Ironically, the *ss Great Britain* ran out of Liverpool, the terminus

of the supposedly bumpy inter-city railway built by his rival George Stephenson, rather than Bristol, a primary reason being the refusal of the harbour authorities to make further improvements such as widening the gates to the Floating Harbour.

After running aground in Dundrum Bay in Ireland on September 22, 1846, her owners could not afford the repair bill and sold the *ss Great Britain* to Liverpool shipping firm Bright, Gibbs & Co for a knockdown $18,000.

The Great Western Steamship Company was wound up in February 1852.

Chapter 5

The Tramway Bridge was built to carry William James' tramway across the River Avon to Stratford's Bancroft Basin. ROBIN JONES

THE FORGOTTEN FATHER OF RAILWAYS

Four years before George Stephenson's Liverpool & Manchester Railway, *Rocket* and all, carried its first passengers, and nearly a decade before Isambard Kingdom Brunel began work as engineer to the Great Western Railway, the first part of a planned inter-city transport link opened in Warwickshire.

The Central Junction Railway was planned to run from Stratford-upon-Avon to London and at 100 miles would, at least in its early years, have become the longest horse-drawn tramway of them all. Only 16 miles of it was built, and the man behind it, coalmaster William James – whose ideas for other lines were taken up by the likes of Stephenson, but was never given credit for them – died in obscurity, and only now have historians started to acknowledge his achievements.

A Stratford & Moreton Tramway horse-drawn wagon on display in the Great Hall of the National Railway Museum at York. ROBIN JONES

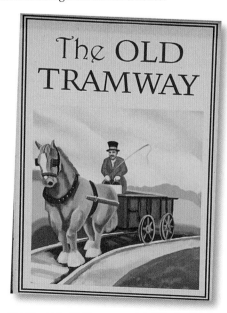

The sign of the Old Tramway pub in Shipston Road, Stratford-upon-Avon, recalls the early horse-drawn railway built by William James, and which ran behind the premises to Moreton-in-Marsh and Shipston-on-Stour. ROBIN JONES

UNJUSTLY IGNORED

MILLIONS of people in Britain are familiar with the names Isambard Kingdom Brunel and George Stephenson, even if they are not interested in railways and civil engineering.

However, if you asked people in the street who in the field of railways was William James, virtually none of them would have any idea.

Yet James pre-dated both Brunel and the Stephensons, and had embarked on building a tramway/canal hybrid system to link Birmingham and the Black Country to London, which at 100 miles would have become the world's first inter-city railway.

Indeed, many historians now believe solicitor's son William James, who was born in Henry-in-Arden, Warwickshire in 1771, and not *Rocket* inventor George Stephenson, is the true father of modern railways. However, popular history has unjustly ignored him in favour of his more illustrious counterparts.

James was the second of the seven children of William James, a lawyer and Justice of the Peace from Moseley in Birmingham, and his wife Mary, who came from a wealthy and well-connected family in nearby Kings Norton. James was educated at the King's School, Warwick, and also in Birmingham's Winson Green.

On September 4, 1793, in the village of Wootton Wawen, a mile south of Henley-in-Arden, James married Dinah Tarleton, the daughter of local landowners.

Henley's 15th century Guildhall, where William James was High Bailiff from 1801 to 1819. ROBIN JONES

LEFT: The William James memorial plaque on the front of the Yew Tree, a Grade II-listed building. ROBIN JONES

The couple settled at the Yew Trees, a house in High Street, Henley-in-Arden, and enjoyed a high social standing locally, mixing socially with landowners and aristocracy from across the county.

After training and qualifying as a solicitor at Lincoln's Inn in London, James returned to Henley-in-Arden around 1797 to work in his father's law firm.

The share price collapse that accompanied the economic panic of 1797 led to increased financial pressures both for the family and the solicitors' practice, so the following year the younger William James started a new career as a land agent, initially managing the estate of the Dewes family of Wellesbourne Hall.

In this role he supervised estates in the West Midlands and beyond for,

A contemporary portrait of early railway protagonist, colliery owner and land agent William James, from an engraving by W Roffe.

among others, the Dewes family of Wellesbourne Hall, Warwickshire; the Earl of Warwick, of Warwick Castle; the Yates family of Lancashire; the Earl of Dartmouth at Sandwell Park, West Bromwich; the Archbishop of Canterbury at Lambeth in London; and the Agar family of Lanhydrock House in Cornwall.

As an early business venture, James sought unsuccessfully for seams of coal in East Sussex, but as his personal fortune grew, he bought a colliery in south Staffordshire and was the first to open a mine in the West Bromwich coalfield, paving the way for the exploitation of the mineral reserves of what became the Black Country.

The house in High Street, Henley-in-Arden where William James lived was known as Yew Tree Hall because of eight trees in the garden planted in the early-18th century. It later became a hotel. ROBIN JONES

Wootton Wawen Aqueduct as seen from above water level. ROBIN JONES

PLANNING THE FIRST INTER-CITY RAILWAYS

However, James had much bigger visions than the building of a waterway linking the River Avon with industrial Birmingham.

Railways had largely preceded canals, but until the 19th century were little more than short 'add ons' over which horses hauled wagons down to the nearest barge loading point or harbour.

The invention of the steam locomotive by Trevithick and its first successful public demonstration on the Penydarren Tramroad, near Merthyr

STARTING WITH A WATERWAY

Having a knowledge of geology, James often advised his clients to concentrate on realising the mineral wealth of their estates, and it was in this connection he first began to propose railways, including, in 1802/03, an early version of the Bolton & Leigh Railway, which in 1828 became the first public railway in Lancashire.

Around 1806, James conjectured the horse-drawn railways that had been a common means of transporting goods in and around collieries for almost two centuries could form the basis of a national system of public transportation.

Railways, of course, had existed for centuries or more before the invention of the steam locomotive: their origin has been said to date back to the theatres of ancient Greece, when parallel grooves carved in stage floors were used as a quick and highly efficient means of moving scenery. The Romans had private railways, but those were worked by horses or manpower, as was the case in the UK in the very early Industrial Revolution.

Uniquely among early railway

pioneers, James saw the potential of railways for rapidly transporting passengers as well as goods and minerals. It is believed by some that in 1808, James attended Cornish mining engineer Richard Trevithick's demonstration of his locomotive *Catch Me Who Can* on a circle of track ironically near the future site of Euston station. William James became chairman of the West Bromwich Coalmasters Association, and was a leading proponent of the development of the local canal system.

Despite his vision for railways as the future of transport, he became deputy chairman and the major shareholder of the company which built the 25.3-mile Stratford-upon-Avon Canal from King's Norton, where it split off from the Worcester & Birmingham Canal, to Kingswood Junction Lapworth. Here, it met the Grand Union Canal before diverging again and carrying on to Stratford.

James was responsible for the iron aqueducts on the southern section, and a plaque on the side of the aqueduct

which crosses the A3400 at Wootton Wawen, next to the Navigation pub, records the fact.

He also directed the building of the next one along – Bearley Aqueduct – constructed by William Whitmore. It remains the longest canal aqueduct in Britain. The third iron structure is the modest Yarningale Aqueduct, which carries the canal over a small stream near Preston Bagot. It was built in 1834 to replace the original wooden structure, which was washed away when the stream flooded that year.

Building work on the canal began in 1893 and it finally opened to Stratford on June 24, 1816. James' investments in collieries and the canal made him a rich man, and it had been estimated by 1815 he was already worth £150,000.

He was also Deputy Recorder for Warwick from 1801, Commandant of the Warwick Defence Volunteers from 1801 to 1804, and remained as land agent to the Earl of Warwick until 1814. He owned much property in Warwick and rented offices in its High Street, now covered by the Aylesford restaurant and hotel.

The Stratford-upon-Avon Canal has for decades been one of Britain's most popular waterways for barge holidays. Here, a pleasure boat is seen heading from Hockley Heath in Solihull towards Illshaw Heath. ROBIN JONES

Wootton Wawen Aqueduct, which was engineered by William James, carries the Stratford-upon-Avon Canal over the A3400 in an iron trough. Built under the direction of James, it was completed in 1813.

A major engineering feature on the northern half of the Stratford-upon-Avon Canal is this brick-built viaduct spanning the valley of the River Cole and the appropriately named Aqueduct Road, north of Major's Green, near Shirley. ROBIN JONES COLLECTION

One of the features of the Stratford-upon-Avon Canal are winch-operated drawbridges, such as this example to the east of Hockley Heath. ROBIN JONES

Tydfil, in 1804, and its subsequent development in the coalfields of north-east England in the decade that followed, was to change all that.

Inspired by the Industrial Revolution and its world-changing inventions, James saw Stratford-upon-Avon's Bancroft Basin, where the canal met the navigable Upper Avon, in which James also held shares, as the hub of a major nationwide transport system, a sort of 'Spaghetti Junction' of its day.

As a mine owner, he had watched the development of horse-drawn tramways and early railways to carry coal from the pithead to the nearest canal for shipment across the country.

In 1815, at the time of the Napoleonic Wars, he wrote to the Prince Regent proposing a railway link between the two principal naval dockyards at Chatham and Portsmouth, which in peacetime could be used for passenger traffic. During the Napoleonic Wars, James served as an officer in the Warwickshire Regiment of Yeomanry Cavalry.

He drew up wildly ambitious plans for a 100-mile Central Junction Railway linking the basin to Paddington, London via Moreton-in-Marsh, Oxford, Thame and Uxbridge – and although the mode of transport had still not caught on by then, he dared to suggest, once his survey for the ambitious route was completed in 1820, it would make use of steam locomotives.

James met locomotive pioneers George and Robert Stephenson and the iron founder William Losh at Killingworth Colliery, Northumberland, in 1821, during one of several trips he

RESERVOIRS BUILT TO 'FEED' CANAL

In order to supply water to the Stratford-upon-Avon Canal, in the 1820s three reservoirs were built by damming two streams at Earlswood Common near Tanworth-in-Arden. The construction of the 25-acre Earlswood Lakes took nearly five years to complete, and the labour force included prisoners of war from the Napoleonic Wars.

The lakes proved attractive to visitors from Birmingham from the early-1900s, and their popularity has been maintained.

The three reservoirs are called Engine Pool, Windmill Pool and Terry's Pool, and a Grade II-listed engine house is located beside the Engine Pool. Its purpose was to pump water into a mile-long canal feeder arm to the canal.

The lakes still supply the canal, and also provide leisure facilities, including sailing, fishing and walking. To the west, the lakes are bounded by a Site of Special Scientific Interest, Clowes Wood and New Fallings Coppice, while Terry's Pool, the most secluded of the three, is a nature reserve. ROBIN JONES

made to study railways in the local coalfield.

This meeting led to an agreement for James to market the Stephenson/Losh patent locomotive (which James branded as the Land-Agent type) in England, south of the Humber-Mersey line, with a supplementary agreement for Stephenson and Losh to use the patent for multi-tubular locomotive boilers taken out by William Henry James, William James's son.

James and George Stephenson also agreed to build what would have been the world's first inter-city railway, between Liverpool and Hull, but were unable to get the project of the ground.

However, James had even more railway plans, this time for a line linking Liverpool to Manchester. He had suggested building a line between the

The road on the top of the Earlswood Lakes dam with the brick engine house in the distance. ROBIN JONES

Traditional canal barge ware to the fore at Kingswood Junction today. ROBIN JONES

This distinctive barrel-shaped lock keeper's cottage at Lapworth is typical of others on the southern 'half' of William James' Stratford-upon-Avon Canal. ROBIN JONES

two cities as early as 1803, and produced his preliminary survey for the route in 1822.

He received the backing of wealthy Liverpool Quaker merchant Joseph Sandars, and also drew up plans for many other railways around Britain.

In 1822, on behalf of Sandars, William James, with his brother-in-law Paul Padley as chief surveyor, began to survey a route for the Liverpool & Manchester Railway. Busy with his canals and collieries, James hired Stephenson to survey the best route.

In 1823/24, James surveyed three possible routes for the Canterbury & Whitstable Railway. He also advocated railways as an extension to the Grand Surrey Canal and as an alternative to the proposed, but never built, London & Cambridge Junction Canal; and steam locomotives for the Surrey Iron Railway.

However, George Stephenson was never prepared to produce locomotives for James to demonstrate to potential clients therefore no sales were made through his agency.

Standing next to the Stratford-upon-Avon Canal in Salter Street, near Earlswood, is the huge red-brick Victorian Gothic St Patrick's church, a significant landmark which can be seen over the fields for miles around. It is built near the site of a wayside chapel that existed in the Middle Ages, but which subsequently disappeared without trace. The present church had its beginnings in 1825 when the company which built the Stratford-upon-Avon Canal took 51 acres of land at Earlswood Common to create Earlswood Lakes. At the same time, residents of the scattered hamlets of the district began calling for a place of worship which would be much nearer to them than the parish church at Tanworth-in-Arden. So the money raised from the sale of the common land to the canal company was used to provide a church in Salter Street, the main road between Earlswood, Shirley and Solihull. An Anglican parish church, it has long been suggested it was dedicated to St Patrick because it would appeal to the Catholic Irish navvies building the canal. It was rebuilt in its present form in 1899 and still isolated. ROBIN JONES

Kingswood Junction at Lapworth is the 'halfway point' on the Stratford-upon-Avon Canal, where it meets the Grand Union Canal. ROBIN JONES

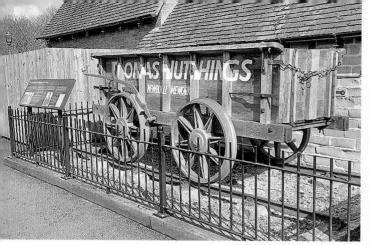

Another of the Stratford & Moreton Tramway's horse-drawn wagons, which belonged to Thomas Hutchings, of Newbold Lime Works, Newbold-on-Stour, was restored and is now displayed near the southern end of Tramway Bridge in Stratford-upon-Avon. The trackbed on the tramway is now a public footpath behind properties in Shipston Road. PHILIP HALLING*

GREAT WESTERN RAILWAY SUCCESSORS TO STRATFORD & MORETON RAILWAY COMPANY

THIS OLD WAGON STANDING ON A LENGTH OF THE ORIGINAL TRACK CHAIRS AND STONE BLOCKS OF THE 4' 8½" GAUGE WAS FORMERLY USED ON THE TRAMWAY OR RAILROAD BETWEEN STRATFORD-UPON-AVON AND MORETON-IN-MARSH. THE TRAMWAY WAS AUTHORISED BY PARLIAMENT IN 1821 AND WAS OPENED IN SEPTEMBER 1826, AND A BRANCH LINE TO SHIPSTON-ON-STOUR OPENED IN 1836.

ONE OF THE EARLIEST SCHEMES OF RAILWAY DEVELOPMENT IN THE UNITED KINGDOM IT WAS PROJECTED, SURVEYED AND LARGELY FINANCED BY WILLIAM JAMES OF HENLEY-IN-ARDEN 1771-1837, A FARSIGHTED ENGINEER, SURVEYOR AND LAND AGENT WHO WAS IN WHOLE OR IN PART RESPONSIBLE FOR MANY OTHER RAILWAY AND CANAL SCHEMES INCLUDING THE STRATFORD CANAL.

THE LINE REMAINED OPEN MAINLY FOR FREIGHT TRAFFIC UNTIL THE LATTER PART OF THE LAST CENTURY AND THE TRACK WAS TAKEN UP IN THE GREAT WAR. THE BRANCH FROM SHIPSTON-ON-STOUR TO MORETON-IN-MARSH, CONVERTED TO STEAM IN 1889 CLOSED IN 1960.

THIS WAGON AFTER RETIREMENT WAS USED AS A CHICKEN COOP AT ITS OWNER'S FARM IN ALDERMINSTER AND HAS SINCE STOOD ON THIS SPOT FOR SOME THIRTY YEARS. THE WAGON WAS RESTORED IN THE SUMMER OF 1971 BY STUDENTS OF THE ENGINEERING DEPARTMENT OF THE SOUTH WARWICKSHIRE COLLEGE OF FURTHER EDUCATION AND THE PLINTH CAST AND THE TRACK RE-LAID BY MEMBERS OF THE STRATFORD & MORETON TRAMWAY COMMITTEE.

NO CREDIT GIVEN FOR 'BORROWED' IDEAS

In 1822/23, James was jailed for debt in the King's Bench Prison in Southwark. His problem had been taking on too much.

In the early 1820s, he had become involved with speculative railway schemes in Kent, Cambridgeshire and Surrey, and ran out of money as he travelled all over the country.

He was declared bankrupt in 1823, a situation compounded by bouts of illness, and had to give up his work on the Liverpool & Manchester Railway, leaving the door wide open for George Stephenson just as the railway age began. While behind bars, he spent his time drawing up a scheme for a network of railways in the south of England, and after he was discharged from prison he returned to his earlier profession as land agent.

However, in his absence, Sandars had formed the Liverpool & Manchester Railway Company – and invited Stephenson to produce a new survey for it, with Padley's assistance. In 1824, Stephenson was appointed surveyor to the line, and his survey for the route largely followed that which had already been proposed by the now somewhat discredited James. And it was Stephenson's report, not that of James, which in 1826 impressed Parliament, for MPs to sanction the building of the line.

In 1825, Stephenson was appointed engineer to the Canterbury & Whitstable Railway, using James's least-preferred route, but taking the credit himself.

However, one of James's transport schemes started to bear fruit.

On September 5, 1826, the northernmost 16 miles of his Central Junction Railway opened as the horse-worked Stratford & Moreton Tramway, and became the first railway to be built in Warwickshire. The parliamentary act for the line had been passed in 1821, with the engineers who built the line being George Stephenson's brother Robert senior and John Urpeth Rastrick, one of the first English steam locomotive builders. While in partnership with John Hazledine, in Bridgnorth, Rastrick had helped Trevithick develop his ideas for the high-pressure steam engine and locomotive, and constructed the locomotive that had been demonstrated in London in 1808.

In 1827, James moved to Bodmin in Cornwall primarily to improve the estates of Anna-Maria Agar of Lanhydrock. He had plans to develop the ports of Devoran and Truro and build a railway from Fowey to Padstow, none of which came to fruition. Following a winter journey by mail coach he contracted pneumonia and died at Bodmin in early 1837, three years after Cornwall's first steam-operated line opened – the Bodmin & Wadebridge Railway.

He never did manage to link Fowey and Padstow by rail, but the GWR and North Cornwall Railway (London & south Western Railway) built branches to each, respectively. The GWR also had

The entrance driveway to Springfield House, to the south of Stratford, crosses this Grade II-listed bridge over the trackbed of the Stratford & Moreton Tramway. MICHAEL DIBB*

running rights from Bodmin to Padstow, where the station opened on March 27, 1899.

The Stratford & Moreton Tramway saw neither London nor steam locomotives, and relied throughout its existence on horses to pull the trains.

Only the route to Moreton from Stratford and one of the three planned branches, that to Shipston-on-Stour, was built.

On a local basis, apart from James' grandiose dreams of a transport artery linking Birmingham, the West Midlands and London, the tramway and canal were intended to carry Black Country coal to the rural districts of south Warwickshire, and limestone and agricultural produce northwards.

Freight on the tramway was conveyed by licensed traders in their own wagons, who were also allowed to convey passengers on payment of a further licence, costing £12 a year.

The Shipston branch was delayed because the original powers expired before it could be built, and so it was not opened until February 11, 1836.

LOSSES INCREASED

The arrival of the Oxford, Worcester & Wolverhampton Railway cut off the Moreton terminal buildings from the branch, forcing it to take out a perpetual lease from May 1, 1847.

The Oxford, Worcester & Wolverhampton upgraded the entire length of the tramway so it could handle main line wagons. Although it has been claimed there were experiments with steam locomotives on the tramway at this time, these main line wagons were still horse drawn.

This innovation did not bring any turnaround in fortunes for the tramway; quite the opposite as its losses increased.

Lingering hopes the tramway to Stratford could become a financial success evaporated in 1859 with the opening of the Oxford, Worcester & Wolverhampton Honeybourne to Stratford via Long Marston branch.

The lock entrance to Stratford's Bancroft Basin from the River Avon. Here was the northern terminus of the Stratford & Moreton Tramway. Had the tramway reached London, as William James intended, it would have become a cauldron of activity as goods were transferred from wagon to barge for onwards shipment. ROBIN JONES

At last, Stratford had a direct rail connection to London, but not the one James designed and had started building.

In 1859, the tramway branch between Moreton and Shipston was converted into a 'proper' railway.

The GWR took over the Oxford, Worcester & Wolverhampton in 1863. The tramway company went bankrupt in 1868, and the line was then taken over by the GWR.

In 1882, a short spur at Longdon Road station was constructed to enable through running to Shipston-on-Stour. This move was part of the GWR's strategy to bring the six-mile Shipston branch up to a standard sufficient to handle steam hauled traffic.

Further statutory powers were sought after the GWR found the original 1833 Act, which gave assent for the branch, banned the use of steam locomotives, and it was not until July 1, 1889 the line was officially reopened with a service of four trains per day in each direction.

Although shorter lengths of the tramway were used by locals, the tramway's through service to Stratford infrequently saw trains, and the line – which had been built to the Stephenson gauge of 4ft 8½in – largely fell into disuse by the mid-1880s and altogether in 1904, its rails finally being ripped up for the war effort in 1918.

However, it was not until August 4, 1926, a month short of its centenary, that the line was officially abandoned by an Act of Parliament.

The GWR withdrew its passenger services from the Shipston branch on July 8, 1929, but freight traffic continued until May 2, 1960.

Partly because he was never acknowledged by George Stephenson, James received little recognition for his work and was by and large quickly forgotten. However, in recent years, efforts have been made to resurrect James and his unfairly soured reputation.

A commemorative plaque has been

A bridge which once carried the Stratford & Moreton Tramway. DAVID STOWELL*

Many of the original stone sleepers from William James's tramway can still be found along its route. The two holes were for fastening the rail, and the faint line running perpendicularly between them is a wear mark from the rail itself. DAVID STOWELL*

Stratford's centrepiece Bancroft Basin, entered by the Stratford-upon-Avon Canal on the far side. Had William James's plans to build a tramway from here to London succeeded, this spot could have become a Clapham Junction of the early railway world! Today, it is a popular haunt of tourists and picnickers. ROBIN JONES

The Harbour, Padstow

William James began drawing up plans for a coast-to-coast railway between the Cornish ports of Fowey and Padstow (pictured in 1910), but died from pneumonia before he could take his scheme further.
ROBIN JONES COLLECTION

installed on the wall of Yew Tree House, the 16th-century Henley-in-Arden property where he and his wife spent the early years of their marriage. The couple sold it in 1802 when they moved to Wellesbourne. However, it was not until 2007 a major biography of William James was published, by which time a huge amount of material had appeared on his contemporaries Brunel and the Stephensons.

A road, William James Way, is named after him in the David Wilson Henley Point Development in Henley-in-Arden.

The finest legacy of James's line is the multi-arch Tramway Bridge, in the heart of Stratford, a landmark famous the world over because of international visitors using it to walk across the River Avon in the town where William Shakespeare was born, and which is the home of the Royal Shakespeare Theatre.

The A3400 from Stratford-upon-Avon still has wide verges on one side or the other for several miles south of the town. These wide verges used to accommodate the tramway. DAVID STOWELL*

RIGHT: BR Standard 2MT 2-6-0 No. 78009 shunts at Shipston-on-Stour station on April 26, 1960, shortly before the closure of the branch, which marked the last page in the history of William James's Stratford & Moreton Tramway. GEOFFREY SKELSEY*

Chapter 6

Seeking an alternative to steam

Even before the steam locomotive had evolved into anything resembling its 'modern' form, inventors were already looking at alternatives which could be more efficient and effective. One of the best-known schemes was Isambard Kingdom Brunel's short-lived South Devon atmospheric railway, a major relic of which was rediscovered in April 2018. Even before Stephenson's *Rocket* appeared, Brunel was experimenting with a locomotive that could be powered by a chemical reaction. However, in trying to better the steam locomotive concept or even replace it outright, Brunel had many rivals both before and long, long afterwards.

Most people could name an Isambard Kingdom Brunel masterpiece, if only the Clifton Suspension Bridge or *SS Great Britain*, and not the Royal Albert Bridge, Bristol Temple Meads station or Box Tunnel.

We thought we knew them all, but in April 2018, another massive structure believed to have been his work was rediscovered, right under our noses, or rather, right under the village of Starcross, in south Devon.

Two 105ft-long and 10ft-wide caverns with a spectacular display of stalactites, formed by dripping water from the roof, and linked by 120 arches, were discovered purely by chance as workmen carried out a £4million Environment Agency flood defence scheme in the seaside village.

The Environment Agency's

contractors found that a manhole led to the large underground chamber beneath a car park.

It was believed to be an underground reservoir associated with Brunel's South Devon atmospheric railway, one of the more unusual chapters in the history of Britain's national network. Basically, the South Devon Railway as originally engineered by him had no locomotives, but had trains which were pulled along by a vacuum in a huge pipe between the rails.

In turn, the vacuum was created by giant stationary steam engines located in pump houses placed at intervals along the route between Exeter and Totnes/Torquay.

Because of the national significance of the surprise discovery, work on a Devon County Council road-widening

scheme above the chamber was stopped, and was thought unlikely to resume. Highways experts were having to go back to the drawing board because of the find.

Brunel's atmospheric railway began operations in September 1847, and although it was designed to conquer the gradients of the foothills of Dartmoor, where it was thought conventional steam locomotives would struggle, the idea of introducing an entirely new form of main line traction at that time was certainly revolutionary.

Of course, while we know Richard Trevithick kicked off the steam railway age with his inventions of 1802 and 1804, nothing was ever cast in stone to state the steam locomotive was the last word in train travel.

Indeed, while George Stephenson,

The pumping station at Dawlish – with the vacuum pipe running between the rails – in a painting by the English landscape painter Nicholas Condy.

LEFT: A contemporary sketch of a South Devon Railway atmospheric train.

The sweeping vista of red sandstone cliffs penetrated by Brunel's vacuum-operated railway, with a pumping station in the distance.

Timothy Hackworth and others were taking Trevithick's concept to the next stage, Isambard was carrying out research of his own into an alternative to the steam locomotive, in the form of the Gaz engine.

In the early-1820s, Isambard and his father Marc investigated ways in which to produce a new and better form of engine power than steam, powered by liquefied carbon dioxide.

Around that time, Isambard was working as assistant engineer on his father's project to build the Thames Tunnel. He used the redundant tunnelling works at Rotherhithe to further his experiments with the Gaz engine.

Originally his father's idea, the aim was to develop an engine that ran on power generated from alternately heating and cooling carbon dioxide made from ammonium carbonate and sulphuric acid.

The scheme was to generate gas from carbonate of ammonia and sulphuric acid and pass it into two surface condensers that were alternately heated and cooled and which communicated through expansion vessels and valves with a power cylinder. When the gas in one condenser was held in its condensed state by passing cold water through the condenser tubes and the other was heated by the circulation of hot water, the difference in pressure between the two vessels was 35 atmospheres. This was the power that Brunel endeavoured to harness, and which he believed at the time might supersede the power of steam.

The technical problems which had to be solved in order to translate theory into practice were immense and that they were solved is in itself was extraordinary, considering the very limited metallurgical knowledge at that time.

The gas condensed at a pressure of no less than 300 atmospheres, while pipes and pipe joints had to be made to withstand pressures of 1500lbs per sq in – in an age when, in steam engineering, 50lbs per sq in was often considered dangerously high. Cast iron was obviously useless and a type of gunmetal was eventually evolved for the pressure vessels.

During his experiments, Isambard might have been the first person to convert carbon dioxide (gas) into its solid form (dry ice).

At Rotherhithe, Brunel spent six months working with an assistant named Withers on the project. There was interest from several parties, including the Admiralty, which gave grant-aid funding.

In his 1957 volume Isambard Kingdom Brunel, the transport historian L T C Rolt, who founded the Talyllyn Railway Preservation Society and spearheaded the volunteer-led drive to run the world's first heritage railway, wrote: "Brunel's notes and sketches suggest an apparatus just about as safe as a ticking time-bomb, and the most remarkable thing is that he and Withers failed to blow themselves up!

"At long last, however, Brunel was forced to admit defeat. On January 30th 1833 he wrote 'Gaz - After a number of experiments I fear we must come to the conclusion that (with carbonic acid at least) no sufficient advantage on the score of economy of fuel can be obtained over steam power'."

So after 10 years of experiments, and a small fortune spent in vain, Isambard gave up on the Gaz engine. However, the failure did not close his mind to alternatives to the steam railway locomotive by any means.

A 5in-gauge working scale model of a Brunel atmospheric railway train, built by Barometer World at Merton in North Devon, a firm whose business is based around the concept of air pressure.
BAROMETER WORLD

MY FIRST BRUNEL ENCOUNTER

From a very early age, I was a railway fanatic, thanks to my elder brother Stewart. I can recall being pushed the one-and-a-half miles to Widney Manor station on the Birmingham Snow Hill to Leamington line in a pram, and spending hours trainspotting.

Back in the early Sixties, if you were a schoolboy, you were not exactly spoiled for choice for ways to spend your spare time. There was no internet, no computer games, no electronic gadgets – in the school holidays, you either kicked a football around on the estate green, went bird nesting, collecting a jam-jar aquarium, or went trainspotting (if you were lucky enough to live near an airport, you could go plane spotting).

Each sunny day in the school holidays, most stations along the line would have a gathering of schoolboys with their Ian Allan locospotters' books, eagerly underlining each number as a steam locomotive passed.

At the age of four, our parents took us to Waterside caravan park at Goodrington, near Paignton. The GWR Kingswear branch (now the Dartmouth Steam Railway) passed over a footpath leading from the adjacent site to the little rocky beach.

The next year, we had an apartment in the heart of Goodrington, a short walk not only to Goodrington Halt, but also to the beach, where there was a wonderful miniature railway on which I rode several times. It disappeared decades ago.

While Stewart and I would seize any chance to visit the big railway, coming back from the station with pockets full of timetable leaflets, we were totally oblivious to one of the most import pieces of railway history right under our noses.

The beach was for sandcastling and taking pedallos out to sea. I enjoyed digging water channels to fill the moats around my sandcastles, but my mum stopped me from going anywhere near a pool that had formed at the end of what looked like an enormous ribbed steel sewage outlet pipe. Fast forward nearly 40 years, and after I launched Heritage Railway magazine, I visited the Great Western society's Didcot Railway Centre and was given a guided tour. One outdoor display was that of a large ribbed pipe, which seemed vaguely familiar.

I was told it had been part of Brunel's atmospheric railway….and yes, it was that very pipe from Goodrington Sands – only my well-meaning and protective mum was wrong in that it never carried sewage, but had been installed as a culvert to take a clean freshwater stream out on to the beach.

A VACUUM BIGGER THAN A HOOVER!

After completing the Bristol & Exeter Railway, Brunel had Plymouth in his sights and was appointed engineer of the South Devon Railway, which was also to be built to 7ft¼in broad gauge. The planned route would cross the foothills of Dartmoor, with steep gradients which would later become legendary in the records of Great Western Railway locomotive feats – Hemerdon, Dainton and Rattery. However, as stated previously, Brunel had doubts the steam locomotives of the day would be up to the job.

In September 1844, Brunel and his locomotive engineer Daniel Gooch, witnessed a demonstration by shipbuilders and inventors Samuel Clegg, a gas lighting pioneer, and Jacob Samuda, a marine engineering expert, of an 'atmospheric' train on Ireland's 1½-mile long Dalkey & Kingstown Railway.

The pair, both members of the Institution of Civil Engineers, had patented their new system of propulsion on January 3, 1838.

They built a full-scale model at Southwark in London, and in 1840 leased half a mile of track on the West London Railway at Wormholt Scrubs (later Wormwood Scrubs), where the railway had not yet been opened to the public. Shortly afterwards, Clegg left for Portugal, where he was pursuing his career in the gas industry.

Their system comprised a cast-iron tube laid between rails and sealed by airtight valves at each end. The leading vehicle in a train was a piston carriage, which carried a piston inserted in the

Arriving at Kingstown on Ireland's Dalkey Atmospheric Railway in 1844.

tube. A piston linked to the bottom of a carriage was pushed past the vale into the tube, and the huge stationary steam engines pumped air out of the tube, generating a vacuum ahead of the piston.

The greater pressure of the atmosphere behind the piston would force it along the tube and pull the carriage with it, eliminating the need for an engine. Indeed, it was basically a giant version of a domestic vacuum cleaner.

The Wormwood Scrubs demonstration ran for two years.

At the time, there was huge public interest in the concept of such atmospheric railways, and several other inventors such as James Pilbrow, Henry Lacey and Joseph Shuttleworth drew up their own plans.

In 1841 Joseph Samuda published A Treatise on the Adaptation of Atmospheric Pressure to the Purposes of Locomotion on Railways, and April 1844 saw Jacob Samuda and his brother Joseph take out a patent for their system. Soon afterwards Joseph died, and it was left to his brother to continue the work.

The standard gauge Dublin & Kingstown Railway opened in 1834 connecting the port of Dún Laoghaire (then called Kingstown) to Dublin, and six years later plans were made to extend it to Dalkey, a distance of about two miles. It used part of the Dalkey Quarry industrial tramway, which was earlier used for the construction of Kingstown Harbour.

It was the first railway of its type in the world. Steeply graded at 1-in-115, with a 440-yard stretch of 1-in-57, and heavily curved, the sharpest being 570 yards radius, difficulties with steam locomotives were foreseen.

James Pim, the treasurer of the company, viewed Samuda's line and thought it to be perfect for the requirements of the Dalkey branch. With the help of a government loan of £26,000, it was installed on what became the Dalkey Atmospheric Railway.

August 19, 1843, saw the line opened to the public, with speeds of 30mph reached to Dalkey, and the train returning back to Kingstown by gravity.

The ground-breaking and headline-grabbing atmospheric railway attracted the attention of eminent engineers, such as Robert Stephenson and Isambard Brunel. The Dalkey railway continued to operate successfully for 10 years.

When the system was abolished in 1855 in favour of conventional steam haulage, a 2-2-2 Princess, the first steam engine to be manufactured in Ireland, was operated on the line.

The atmospheric railway pumping station at Dalkey, with its pool of water to supply its steam engine in the foreground.

BRUNEL THE ATMOSPHERIC CONVERT

When Isambard saw atmospheric propulsion at work, he believed he had found the future of rail transport, a new system which was clean, silent and fast, with lighter and more efficient trains. Because atmospheric traction did not depend on the adhesion of heavy locomotives to the rails, he could economise on earthworks, cutting costs while allowing steep inclines. To boost power on the gradients, all you had to do would be to increase the diameter of the vacuum pipe, add a second pipe, or build a bigger pumping engine.

A rare surviving section of the vacuum pipe from Isambard Brunel's atmospheric railway, which for decades was used as a stormwater outfall at Goodrington Sands near Paignton, is now preserved at Didcot Railway Centre, in the middle of a section of broad gauge track. This is one of a batch of 22in pipes ordered to replace the 15in ones in a bid to improve performance, but the system was abandoned before it could be installed. ROBIN JONES

A concrete pipe replaced the section of atmospheric railway vacuum pipe. It had a second life as a steam outfall on Goodrington Sands.

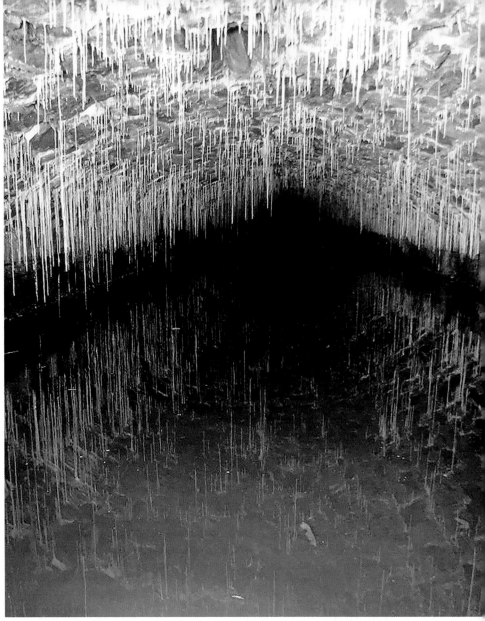

The forgotten cavern beneath Starcross, which is believed to have been built for Isambard Brunel's atmospheric railway pumping station above. The underground reservoir was rediscovered in April 2018 by Environment Agency contractors who lifted a manhole cover. Two 105ft-long and 10ft-wide caverns, with a spectacular display of stalactites formed by dripping water from the roof, and linked by 120 arches, were discovered purely by chance as workmen carried out a £4million tidal flood defence scheme in the seaside village. The Environment Agency began work on the scheme for Starcross and Cockwood in January. ENVIRONMENT AGENCY

The long-demolished pumping station at Newton Abbot highlighting Brunel's Italianate design.

Brunel found a fellow supporter in none other than Prime Minister Sir Robert Peel, who expressed a wish to see all the UK railways adopt the atmospheric system.

During the Railway Mania of the 1840s, railway share prices soared, and anyone wanting to build a new line easily found financial backing.

In the wake of Dublin & Kingstown Railway came more atmospheric railways – the London & Croydon in 1846, the 1.4-mile Paris & St-Germain Railway from Bois de Vezinet to St-Germain in Paris in 1847...and the South Devon Railway.

The latter project received its royal assent on July 4, 1844, and Brunel made plans to build the entire 52-mile line from Exeter to Plymouth as an atmospheric system. One of the biggest contemporary complaints about steam trains – especially in the days of roofless carriages – was they showered passengers with hot water and cinders. By contrast, here was the world's first 'green' transport system – clean, silent and fast.

Nine huge Italianate engine houses were built at three-mile intervals along the route from Exeter to Teignmouth, which in itself was a gargantuan feat of engineering, hugging the foot of storm-lashed cliffs and divided from the sea by a wall, a series of tunnels taking it from one sandy cove to another en route. Indeed, this section, now part of today's national network, is one of the most expensive of all to maintain,

As with so many of his structures, in typical Brunel fashion, he again took the accepted physics of his day and in defying Mother Nature, went one stage further, despite the risk of storm surges from the sea and landslips from the red sandstone cliffs above. This initial stretch opened on May 30, 1846 – using conventional steam locomotives at first, while the vacuum tube and leather and metal valve of the atmospheric system continued to be laid.

At Starcross, Brunel's atmospheric railway engine house became a coal merchants until 1981, with the boiler house containing a Wesleyan Chapel from 1867-1958. The Grade 1-listed building became a museum in 1982. Sadly, the atmospheric caper claimed a second financial victim in 1993 when the excellent museum dedicated to this method of propulsion closed down, following a harsh withdrawal of grant aid at a time when it was attracting a long succession of school parties for educational trips. The fine Italianate sandstone structure, nicknamed 'the tower' by locals, was sold for use as a boat store for the Starcross Fishing and Cruising Club. The tower is about 50ft shorter than when built. READING TOM*

Workmen building the South Devon Railway are depicted laying atmospheric pipes between Totnes and Littlehempston.

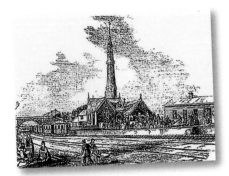

Jolly Sailor station on the London & Croydon Railway in 1845, showing the pumping station and the locomotive-less train. This railway opened with traditional steam locomotive haulage in 1839, was converted to atmospheric population in 1845, and returned to conventional locomotive operation two years later.

FIRST PASSENGERS ENJOY HIGH SPEEDS, BUT...

Two public atmospheric trains ran over the line from September 13, 1847, and from January 10, 1848 services were extended to Newton Abbot, with some freight being carried as well.

The high speeds promised by Brunel were indeed achieved, a very impressive 68mph with a 28-ton load and 35mph with 100 tons.

Nine trains a day ran between Exeter and Teignmouth during the spring and summer of 1848, recording average speeds of 64mph. However, the 20 miles from Exeter to Newton Abbot (with four stops) took a slow 55 minutes because one train had to wait for the other to pass as the route was single track.

However, the system, dubbed 'the Atmospheric caper' by locals, was riddled with problems from the outset.

The great inventor and engineer was held back by the materials available for him to turn his grandiose scheme into a permanent reality. The hinge of the airtight valve and the ring around the piston were both made of leather, an organic material which was totally unsuitable for the purpose, but in the mid-19th century no alternative material was available.

Indeed, the Croydon line scrapped its atmospheric system after repeated breakdowns because of the failure of the valve, but Brunel notoriously failed to mention this to the South Devon board.

Instead, he appointed a large team of

Atmospheric propulsion stages a comeback: the Aeromóvel people carrier at Brazil's international Salgado Filho Airport in Porto Alegre. MARCO PRASS/ARQUIVO TRENSURB

NOT COST EFFECTIVE

Passengers liked the atmospheric trains, until those travelling third class were asked to get out and push when they broke down.

Yet the operating costs did not add up, and far from being a cheaper alternative to steam, the atmospheric system was proving very expensive to run. It cost 37 pence per mile to run an atmospheric train compared to 16 pence for steam.

Angry South Devon Railway directors tracked down the absent Brunel at his home in London's Duke Street. Brunel blamed inventors of the system, and recommended the replacement of the pipes and the steam pumps. Accordingly, the pumps were improved and completely replaced, but to no avail.

On August 29, 1848, in a rare admission of failure, Isambard faced angry shareholders at a meeting in Plymouth and declared he had been wrong about atmospheric propulsion.

With the railway having lost nearly £500,000, and faced with a £25,000 bill to replace the entire valve after less than a year, the railway's board of directors ordered the conversion of the line to steam haulage as from September 10, 1848, or until such time as Clegg & Samuda agreed to repair the airtight valve. That did not happen. The other three lines built to the Clegg and Samuda system were similarly converted for much the same reasons.

Brunel did, however, make one tiny gesture of humility – waiving his fee for overseeing the construction of their railway until it opened throughout to Plymouth on April 2, 1849 as a locomotive-hauled concern, complete with those notorious gradients.

The question remains – what would have been the result had modern adequate materials been available to Brunel? Would the atmospheric system

have killed off the steam locomotive a century before diesel and electric traction did?

Yet, what if the materials to make the atmospheric system work had been available? What if the scheme had been better prepared and proven by in-depth trials before the line was built? Could it have presented a serious competitor to steam haulage more than a century before the advent of diesel and electric locomotive on the British main line?

Nevertheless, the South Devon Railway as a steam line proved hugely successful, and stage by stage was eventually converted to double track throughout in order to handle increasing volumes of traffic. It became part of the GWR on February 1, 1876.

Atmospheric power has not been forgotten. In 2013, an atmospheric people-mover began operation at Brazil's international Salgado Filho Airport in Porto Alegre. Named the Aeromóvel, it is an automated transport system for passengers, which moves along an elevated track. The light-rail vehicle is powered by air generated via industrial fans, which in turn are powered by electricity, and control the pressure, speed and steering.

Only one year of Brunel's broad gauge remained when, in 1981, GWR Rover 4-2-2 *Timour* heads through Teignmouth towards Exeter with 'The Cornishman'. By then, Brunel's atmospheric railway, which ran over this formation, was a distant memory.

men to continually run a sticky sealant on the valve to make it airtight. The sealant was found to be non-effective after exposure to the air, so a new compound comprising cod-liver oil and soap was introduced, but fared no better.

The leather dried and cracked in the sun, wind and salty air, and famously, was said to have been gnawed away by rats, leaving air to leak in through the cracks.

Accordingly, the stationary engines required worked much harder and burned more coal to maintain the necessary pressure in the vacuum pipe.

Two miles of the valve had to be completely replaced, while at the same time the stationary steam engine pumps kept breaking down.

Furthermore, initial tests had shown the planned 12in vacuum pipe needed to be replaced by one of 15in diameter. As a result, the pumping engines already installed along the route had to run faster than their design speed in order to maintain the vacuum.

LIVING ON A KNIFE'S EDGE

With hindsight, perhaps more bizarre than the atmospheric railway concept was the coastal route which Brunel chose, leaving the railway at the mercy of high tides and storm surges, not to mention cliff falls.

In December 1852, a large landslip from the cliffs east of Teignmouth caused the railway to close for four days, and in 1855 and 1859 the sea broke through the line at Teignmouth.

Another serious breach of the railway occurred at Dawlish in October 1865, and again on February 1, 1869, when a 300-yard section of sea wall and track was washed away.

In 1929, the wall between Dawlish and Dawlish Warren was damaged by a

An aerial view of the damage to the railway at Dawlish after the storm of February 4-5, 2014. NETWORK RAIL

storm on Christmas Eve, and there was partial subsidence of the Down line.

The GWR, which used the Teign Valley branch as a diversionary route when necessary from 1903 onwards, announced a scheme for an avoiding line in 1936, even buying land and marking out the route, but the plans were sunk by the Second World War and never revived.

In more recent times, part of the sea wall route in Dawlish was spectacularly washed away on February 4-5, 2014, leaving the double tracks suspended in mid-air. High winds and extremely rough seas led to 130ft of the sea wall and the ballast under the line behind it being washed away.

With Plymouth and Cornwall cut off from the rest of the national network, a £35million repair operation was launched. The repair work was underway before being hampered by

another severe storm on the night of February 14 when huge waves damaged a line of shipping containers forming a breakwater and punched a new hole in the sea wall.

However, a 300-strong Network Rail team managed to get Brunel's sea wall rebuilt within two months.

The first train over the repaired track ran on April 4, in the form of the 5.34am service from Exeter to Paignton.

At Paddington station, sticks of rock were given out to celebrate the line reopening.

They were labelled: "Welcome back Dawlish! The orange army has rebuilt the railway so you can enjoy your journey to the South West again".

Prime Minister David Cameron praised the "Herculean effort" of workers on round-the-clock shifts. He hailed it as "a great day" and said south-west England was "open once again".

At the same time, there was – and still is – widespread clamour for an alternative route to Brunel's coast line to be reopened, such as the Southern Railway main line from Exeter to Plymouth via Okehampton and Tavistock, part of which, between Crediton and Meldeon Quarry, survives as the Dartmoor Railway, a heritage line, and between Plymouth and Bere Alston as Network Rail's Gunnislake branch.

As it was, the two-month closure of the line connecting Devon and Cornwall to the rest of the UK could have cost the South West economy up to £1.2billion, according to a report by the Devon Maritime Forum. It said "all industries were hit" by the storm damage in February 2014.

The first steam locomotive to return over the route which Brunel had

The breach of February 4-5 left both tracks hanging in mid air. NETWORK RAIL

GWR 4-6-0 No. 6024 heads through Dawlish over Brunel's controversial South Devon Railway coastal route in 2012. BARRY LEWIS*

designed with their exclusion in mind came on April 10, 2014, when LNER A4 Pacific No. 60007 *Sir Nigel Gresley* headed a Steam Dreams Woking to Kingswear 'Cathedrals Express' over the rebuilt sea wall section. The BR blue-liveried 4-6-2 made a second crossing on April 19 with the Railway Touring Company's 'Dartmouth Express'.

The public today love travelling over the route between Exeter and Newton Abbot because of its unsurpassed coastal scenery: it has been described as the most beautiful rail route in Britain. Yet there are those who believe Brunel overstepped the mark in its design, and in a world of rising sea levels because of global warming, it is living on borrowed time.

Network Rail's latest solution is to build a 1300ft causeway about 90ft out to sea near Teignmouth to carry the line, at an estimated cost of £500million. The proposals would see the line rebuilt from the tunnel at Smugglers' Lane,

A contemporary sketch of the sea wall breach at Dawlish in 1865.

ABOVE AND RIGHT: Victorian sketches of waves breaking over the railway north of Dawlish, and a rock fall.

Brunel designed his South Devon Railway to be used without steam locomotives. However, after repairs to the major breach at Dawlish in 2014 were completed, one of the most powerful types to run in the UK headed the first two steam-hauled railtours over it. LNER A4 Pacific No. 60007 *Sir Nigel Gresley* is seen heading Steam Dreams' 'Cathedrals Express' over the Dawlish sea wall on April 10 that year. DAVE COLLIER

Waves break against Brunel's sea wall at Dawlish as then Transport Secretary Patrick McLoughlin and Network Rail chief executive Mark Carne view the damage on February 7, 2014. NETWORK RAIL

Nine pumping houses in all were built – at Exeter St Davids, Countess Wear, Turf Locks, Starcross, Dawlish, Bishopsteignton, Newton Abbot, Totnes, and one at Torre, in Torquay – to serve a projected branch line. The last two, which like the one at Starcross, also survive, were never used. Pictured is the Totnes pump house, part of a derelict dairy, which was saved when English Heritage listed it in 2008 following a massive local outcry against imminent demolition. It is now the centre of a major community project, Atmos Totnes. The Totnes Community Development Society is redesigning the former dairy site as a mixed-use development design at the heart of a new centre to boost the town's economy without resorting to green field site development. ROBIN JONES

out on to the beach past Spray Point, and then curve back in land towards Teignmouth.

Transport Secretary Chris Grayling said the Conservative Government was determined to safeguard the line through Dawlish and Teignmouth.

"On top of the £31million put into tackling the damage and disruption caused by the weather in 2014, we have invested a further £15million to enable world-class engineers to design a long-lasting solution for the line."

Brunel exploited the technology of his day to the limit and went one stage beyond. Yet his choice of a route for his atmospheric railway, hugging the cliffs above the tideline, continues to present a problem, as seen in this storm scene from March 2, 2018, when the tracks at Dawlish station were left indurated. NETWORK RAIL

THE WORLD'S FIRST ELECTRIC LOCOMOTIVE

Isambard Kingdom Brunel's adoption of the atmospheric railway system was by no means the only threat to the future of the steam locomotive. Several years before the first atmospheric trains ran from Exeter to Newton Abbot, Scotland saw the world's first electric locomotive.

Highly successful Aberdeen chemist and dyer Robert Davidson built the first known electric locomotive, a model, in 1837.

Educated at Marischal College from 1819-21, he then established a business close to the Aberdeen-Inverurie Canal, at first supplying yeast, before becoming involved in the manufacture and supply of chemicals. He took a deep interest in the embryonic electrical technologies of the day. From 1837, he made small electric motors on his own principles, and in 1839, produced his first car.

In 1840, Davidson was sufficiently confident to stage an exhibition of electrical machinery at Aberdeen in 1840, Edinburgh the next year, and later at the Egyptian Hall in Piccadilly in London. Among the machines on display were electrically operated lathes and printing presses.

The Edinburgh exhibition was visited by the young James Clerk Maxwell, who formulated the classical theory of electromagnetic radiation, bringing together for the first time electricity, magnetism and light as different manifestations of the same phenomenon. Maxwell's equations for electromagnetism have been called the "second great unification in physics" after the first one realised by Isaac Newton – who proved the elliptical orbits of planets could be explained by his laws of motion and a universal gravitational force.

In September 1842, Davidson's full-size electric locomotive, a four-wheeled affair called *Galvani*, powered by zinc-acid batteries, was tested on the Edinburgh to Glasgow line. That was 37 years before Werner von Siemens' electric tramway, often viewed as the first application of electricity to rail motive power, ran at the 1879 Berlin Exhibition. *Galvani* ran at 4mph in the tests, but did not haul any passenger or freight trains.

Sadly, *Galvani* never came to the attention of Brunel: had it done, he would almost certainly have ran the rule over it. Had the potential of the invention been far more widely publicised,

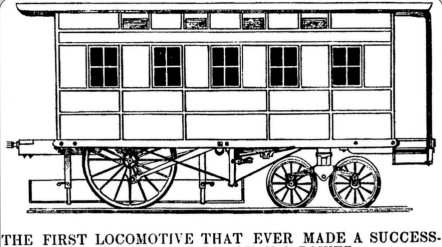

THE FIRST LOCOMOTIVE THAT EVER MADE A SUCCESSFUL TRIP WITH GALVANIC POWER.

Galvani, which in 1842 became the world's first electric locomotive.

Davidson might have overtaken or even eclipsed Brunel's railway achievements.

Local newspaper the Aberdeen Banner had in 1840 already predicted the type of machinery Davidson was producing "will in no distant date supplant steam".

However, unlike Samuda and Clegg's system, no interest in *Galvani* was shown by any of the railway companies of the day, because compared to steam, his electric locomotives were too expensive to manufacture.

As it was, in a display of raw Ludditism, steam apprentices on the Edinburgh & Glasgow Railway felt so threatened by Davidson's electric locomotive they broke into its shed and smashed it to pieces, leaving its sickened inventor to turn away from electric traction, leaving further development to others who came decades later. After 1843, he ceased experiments and for the next half century concentrated on running his chemical business, successfully branching out into perfumes.

It was only when electric

Robert Davidson invented the world's first electric locomotive.

RIGHT: The new replica of one of the motors which powered *Galvani*.
GRAMPIAN TRANSPORT MUSEUM

locomotives were introduced in the 1890s Davidson's achievements in electric traction were recognised. *The Electrician* magazine reported "Robert Davidson was undoubtedly the first to demonstrate the possibility of electrical traction in a practical way".

In 2018, a working replica of what is claimed to be the world's first electric traction motor went on display at the Grampian Transport Museum in Alford, Aberdeenshire. The original was used as one of four, powering *Galvani*.

Museum curator Mike Ward had the motor replica, a replica of the electrical pioneer's 20-cell battery used to power the locomotive, and a model of *Galvani*, built as centrepieces of a new exhibition on electric traction. Mike said: "Until we started to look into Robert Davidson, we hadn't realised just what a significant electric traction pioneer he was.

"Now we're telling his story, which lies at the heart of all electric traction, since his first moving vehicles took to the road and rails, and bringing it up to date with today's developments, which all relate back to Davidson.

"Robert Davidson still deserves to be recognised as the father of electric traction on rails."

BRITAIN'S FIRST ELECTRIC RAILWAY

Isambard Brunel was sent to Brighton to recuperate after narrowly escaping death when the Thames Tunnel excavations flooded on January 12, 1828, killing six workmen.

He spent several months convalescing in Brighton, but his recovery proved slow. When it was discovered 22-year-old Isambard was having 'exertions with actresses', he was dispatched to the

more refined Bristol suburb of Clifton to resume his convalescence. While there, he won a competition to design a suspension bridge over the Avon Gorge, sparking off a chain of events which led to him being chosen as engineer for the Great Western Railway.

However, a second railway revolution was sparked off in Brighton, right on the beach, and had Isambard lived to see it in action, he would almost certainly

have embraced it as a successor to steam As stated previously, the world's first electric passenger train was demonstrated by Siemens in Berlin in 1879. Its locomotive was driven by a 2.2 kW motor which picked up power from a third-rail supply.

It was so successful the firm of Siemens & Halske received inquiries about the investment and operating costs of electric railways from all over the world. However, the city authorities in Berlin were less than enthusiastic, and because of safety concerns, refused to let the firm build elevated electrical railways in Berlin's Friedrichstraße and Leipziger Straße.

Werner von Siemens had to look slightly further afield, and two years later, on May 12, 1881, he opened the world's first electric tram line in the Berlin suburb of Lichterfelde. Regular services began four days later.

Siemens & Halske also converted three horse-drawn streetcar carriages to run on a direct current motor. The two-axle cars, with 16 seats each, carried just under 50 passengers.

Siemens wrote to his brother William in England on May 23: "It is remarkable what effect a ride on the Lichterfelde streetcar has on people. Everyone from the Minister of Labor [Maybach] to the

The electric locomotive demonstrated by Werner von Siemens in 1879 now takes pride of place in the Berlin Technical Museum. ROBIN JONES

Car No. 9 at the western terminus of Aquarium station in 2012. ED WEBSTER*

Rough Sea over Electric Railway, Brighton.

The trestle sections on the Volk's Electric Railway were often hit by storms, just as Brunel's Dawlish sea wall route is still pounded by high tides and storm surges today. The Brighton beach shingle is now much higher and shields the line.

Magnus Volk, who reintroduced the electric railway concept to Britain nearly half a century after Davidson's ill-fated experiments.

simple railway builder is convinced that electric transportation has a great future."

At the first International Electricity Exhibition, held in Paris in August of the same year, Siemens & Halske presented an electric streetcar. The trip in the 50-passenger car from the Place de la Concorde to the Palais de l' Industrie, in the exhibition grounds, proved highly popular with the people of Paris and played a major part in "making the Parisians familiar with" the name of Siemens – as Werner von Siemens wrote in a letter to his brother Carl in Russia.

However, it was not until the Siemens engineer Walter Reichel had in 1889 solved an important constructional problem with the development of the bow collector that the electrical operation of rail vehicles came into its own.

Eight years before Brunel's death, another inventor who was prepared to push the accepted boundaries of physics was born at 35 (now 40) Western Road, Brighton on October 19, 1851.

In 1879, Magnus Volk demonstrated Brighton's first telephone link and became the first resident to install electricity in his home at 38 Dyke Road, the year later.

On August 4, 1883, he unveiled a quarter-mile long, 2ft-gauge electric railway running from a site opposite the town's aquarium to the Chain Pier. Power was provided by a 2hp Otto gas engine driving a Siemens D5 50V DC generator. A small electric car with a 1½hp motor had a top speed of 6mph.

The public instantly took to Volk's railway. Yet Volk did not invent the electric locomotive – that honour had been claimed by Davidson decades before – but he made history by reintroducing the concept to Britain in a workable and commercial format, one which the South Devon atmospheric railway never achieved in its short life.

He subsequently extended his line eastwards from the aquarium to the Banjo Groyne, and the arch at Paston Place, to provide workshop and power facilities, widening the track to 2ft 8½in gauge, and producing two larger and more powerful passenger cars.

The enlarged 1400-yard line opened on April 4, 1884, with a passing loop in the middle.

The line clung to the resort's shoreline, using timber trestles to cross gaps in the shingle, and severe gradients to allow the cars to pass beneath the Chain Pier, but occasional high tides and surges saw the line dice with death in the same way as Brunel's Dawlish sea wall did.

The official opening of Volk's Electric Railway on August 3, 1883.

THE SHIP ON RAILS

Volk became angry at the local council's refusal of permission to extend his line beyond the Banjo Groyne to Rottingdean. So he devised a plan for a truly bizarre form of transport, a cross between a railway, a seaside pier and a ship, which made the Samuda and Clegg atmospheric system adopted by Brunel in South Devon look decidedly common place and normal. The Brighton & Rottingdean Seashore Electric Railway consisted of two parallel 2ft 8½in-gauge tracks, billed as 18ft gauge, the measurement between the outermost rails. The tracks were laid on concrete sleepers mortised into the bedrock 50 yards below the high tide mark.

This single car was a 45ft by 22ft pier-like structure which stood on four 23ft-long legs and weighed 45 tons. It was powered by an electric motor, current being supplied from an overhead pick-up, with masts mounted at regular intervals in the sea.

Officially named *Pioneer*, but many called it 'Daddy Long-Legs'. it needed not only a driver, but a qualified sea captain. Unlike any other train, it was also provided with lifeboats.

This 'railway in the sea', which eclipsed any form of bizarre and unusual transport even Brunel might have devised, was officially opened on November 28, 1896, only to be severely damaged by a storm a week later, when *Pioneer* was turned on to its side.

Repairs completed, it reopened in July 1897, but Volk found himself 'swimming against the tide', for the prevailing current proved too powerful for *Pioneer*, and he could not afford to boost its power. Nearly 45,000 passengers rode on *Pioneer* that year, but all was not well. At high tide, the tram on stilts would slow to a crawl, but the venture had already become a moneypit and upgrading *Pioneer's* motors was out of the question. Plans for a second car were also abandoned.

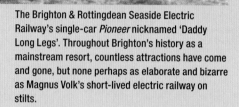

A poster advertising both Brighton electric railways.

The Brighton & Rottingdean Seaside Electric Railway's single-car *Pioneer* nicknamed 'Daddy Long Legs'. Throughout Brighton's history as a mainstream resort, countless attractions have come and gone, but none perhaps as elaborate and bizarre as Magnus Volk's short-lived electric railway on stilts.

In 1901, the local council decided to build a beach protection barrier, and told Volk to divert his line further out to sea. No finance was available, and so the unique electric line through the waves closed forever. In the summer of 1902 the Brighton & Rottingdean Seashore Electric Railway was officially abandoned, less than six years after opening. The infrastructure and *Pioneer* were left to fall into ruin until 1910, eventually being disassembled and sold for scrap. Some of the foundations of it can still be made out at low tide.

A similar contraption had been operating in France for two decades already, although the journey was much shorter and in calmer waters. The French equivalent was pulled by a cable, whereas Volk's version was self-powered, using electricity fed from overhead lines into two, 25hp General Electric motors. Volk's carriage was also much more comfortable. It featured an on-board saloon and promenade deck, upon which passengers could enjoy the view during the 35-minute journey.

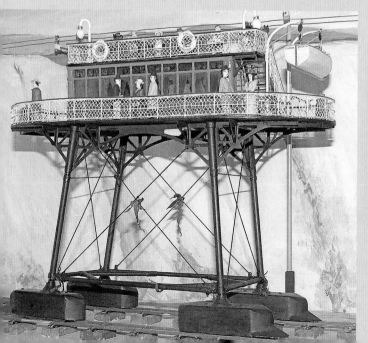

LEFT: *Pioneer*, the 'train' on the Brighton & Rottingdean Seashore Electric Railway, as exhibited at the Model World exhibition at the Brighton Centre in 2006. LES CHATFIELD*

These concrete blocks are the sole remains of the Brighton & Rottingdean Seashore Electric Railway, as seen near the former Rottingdean terminus. Some of the cable poles were still standing in the 1930s. SIMON CAREY*

BACK ON DRY LAND

By the turn of the century, the influence of Magnus Volk had spread far and wide, with the emergence of both electric street trams and electric railways.

The City & South London Railway became the world's first electric underground line when it opened on December 18, 1890. The first section of the Liverpool Overhead Railway opened in 1893, the Mersey Railway was electrified in 1903, the Metropolitan railway 'Inner Circle' in 1905, and the Midland Railway's Morecambe to Heysham line in 1908.

Electrification offered the advantage of rapid acceleration – ideal for urban and suburban lines, which had many stops over a short distance and needed to run intensive timetables – but because of the huge initial outlay, the big railway companies did not consider it an economically viable replacement for steam over their entire networks. We are left to wonder what Isambard Brunel might have thought.

Volk finally won consent to extend his original electric railway to Black Rock, and the new stretch opened in September 1901. Sadly, this was cut back again in 1930 when the council built a new swimming pool.

A new Black Rock station was opened on May 7, 1937 when Volk, then 85, took joint control of Car 10 for a journey. It was his last public appearance as he died peacefully at home 13 days later.

Since 1995, the line, now in the ownership of Brighton City Council, (the local authority having taken it over in 1938) has been supported by local enthusiasts under the banner of the Volk's Electric Railway Association, which on special days run the trains.

Volk's Electric Railway was not the first in the world to run on electricity, but the earlier ones have long since

Car No. 7 at Halfway station in 2009. ROBIN JONES

passed into history, and it was the first in Britain. Therefore of profound historical importance, Britain's electrified main lines and underground railways today can legitimately trace an ancestry back to it. As such it is a national treasure, even though uninformed passers-by might dismiss it as an antique people-carrier from the day before yesteryear.

In 2014, the historically priceless railway was awarded a grant of £1.65million by the Heritage Lottery Fund to build a visitor centre and ticket office at Aquarium station, a new depot with viewing gallery at Halfway station, new conservation workshop and depot at Banjo Groyne, the restoration of cars Nos. 4, 6 and 10 to full working order, and the provision of new educational materials about the railway. The 1983 Centenary Model is displayed inside the visitor gallery. It shows the railway as it was in 1933, including a superb portrayal of the gantry that supported the track over the sea from Banjo Groyne eastwards to Madeira Drive. This gantry

still exists but is buried under the shingle. Traces of it can still be seen.

The railway was temporarily closed for 16 months to allow for the major improvements detailed above. The grand reopening of the railway by TV new reader and volunteer train driver Nicholas Owen took place on Good Friday 2018.

Alan Robins, chairman of Brighton and Hove City Council's tourism, development and culture committee, said: "Magnus Volk was an amazing local inventor and the new workshop and visitor centre are ideal places to learn more about his life and the workings of his trains."

Magnus Volk has also been immortalised in Brighton's Hollywood-style Walk of Fame, the brainchild of resident David Courtney, the man who discovered pop star Leo Sayer in the 1970s.

Isambard Brunel is rightly credited with giving kudos to the atmospheric railway principle by adopting the Samuda and Clegg system for his South

A Volks Electric Railway train nears the eastern terminus on August 27, 2009. ROBIN JONES

One of the two surviving railcars built in 1860 for the Pneumatic Despatch Company, in the care of the National Railway Museum at York. MIKE PEEL*

THE FIRST PNEUMATIC RAILWAY

A permanent 2ft-gauge line in a 4ft-diameter tunnel was laid over a third of a mile between Euston station's Arrival Parcels Office and the North West District Post Office in Eversholt Street. The line was tested from January 15, 1863, and operations began on February 20, 1863. A capsule conveying up to 35 bags of mail could make the short journey between terminals in one minute. A total of 13 journeys were made each day, with a daily operating cost of £1 4s 5d. The Post Office was charged a nominal fee for use of the service.

A contemporary report of the pneumatic line published in 1863 in The Living Age, runs thus: "Near the bottom of Euston Square, there is the mouth of the tube, and there are the travelling trucks, ready to be thrust into it; and as we look, a bell rings at some distance up the rail – this is a signal that a mail-train has arrived... At this signal we hear a shovel of coke thrown into a furnace, a small steam-engine begins to beat swiftly... the pneumatic wheel ... is 21ft in diameter, and is composed of two discs of iron... These discs are braced together by spoke-like partitions, and these partitions communicate with an opening for the entrance of air about the axis.

"As this wheel rapidly revolves, the air is sucked in at its centre, and thrown off ... at its open rim or edge. This gale is not allowed to disperse itself, however, but when any work has to be done, is confined within a paddle-box, and allowed to pass out ... through a pipe in connection with the great pneumatic despatch tube...

"Here, then, we have the means of pulling or pushing the travelling carriages along their subterranean road, and as we speak we see it in operation: for a mail-guard opens a door, throws in two or three mail-bags just snatched out of the guard's van as it rolls into the (main line) station, the iron carriages are shoved into the tube, the air-tight door at its mouth is closed... and we hear them rumbling off on their subterranean

Devon Railway. Yet six years before Isambard was born, and four years before Richard Trevithick gave his first public demonstration of a steam railway locomotive, another inventor had filed a patent for an engine which used compressed air to power vehicles.

Mechanical engineer George Medhurst (1759-1827) pioneered the use of compressed air as a means of propulsion, and it was his ideas that led directly to the development of the first atmospheric railway.

Born in Shoreham, Kent and trained as a clockmaker at Clerkenwell, Medhurst later became interested in pneumatics. In 1799, he filed a patent for a wind pump for compressing air to obtain motive power, and the following year he patented his Aeolian engine.

He went so far as to propose the establishment of Aeolian coach services, operated by pumping stations along the route.

In 1810, he published a paper outlining the potential for using compressed air to carry letters and goods by road. Two years later, he published another paper, calling for passengers and freight to be blown along rails through a tube of 30ft in diameter by the power and velocity of compressed air.

He also envisaged carriages running on railway tracks, propelled by a continuous tube beneath the rails, as would later happen in Ireland and South Devon.

Other inventions by Medhurst included a steam carriage, a 'leak proof' canal lock gate, and a variety of weighing and balancing machines.

Just before his death in September 1827, Medhurst returned to the idea of pneumatic propulsion with his publication of A New System of Inland Conveyance, for Goods and Passengers ... "with the velocity of sixty miles in an hour ... without the aid of horses or any animal power".

Medhurst never lived to see his atmospheric railway idea come to fruition. However, his idea was revived by the London Pneumatic Despatch Company, which was formed on June 30, 1859, with Richard Temple-Grenville, the 3rd Duke of Buckingham and Chandos as chairman, to design, build and operate an underground railway system for the carrying of mail, parcels and light freight between locations in London.

Sir Rowland Hill of the General Post Office commissioned two engineers to investigate the feasibility of a pneumatic tube-based system linking the General Post Office and the West District Central Post Office.

They reported in the mid-1850s that the scheme was feasible, but very costly, and so was not progressed.

However, in 1859, the year of Isambard Kingdom Brunel's death, Thomas Webster Rammell and Josiah Latimer Clark proposed an underground tube network in central London "for the more speedy and convenient circulation of despatches and parcels".

The company was founded with offices at 6 Victoria Street, Westminster. With initial funding of £25,000, (more than £2million by today's equivalent), the company tested the technology and constructed a pilot route at the Soho Foundry of Boulton & Watt in Birmingham.

The first full-scale trial was held in Battersea during the summer of 1861. A single tube was installed, 452 yards long, with curves of up to 300ft radius and gradients of up to 1-in-22. Inside the tube was a 2ft-gauge line.

Wheeled capsules were fitted with vulcanised rubber flaps to make an air seal.

Power was provided by a 30 horse-power steam engine with a 21ft-diameter fan. Single capsules weighed up to three tons, and achieved speeds up to 40mph.

FIRST DESPATCH OF MAIL-BAGS THROUGH THE PNEUMATIC TUBE FROM THE DISTRICT OFFICE IN EVERSHOLT STREET TO EUSTON STATION.

The first mailbags are dispatched from Eversholt Street's district post office to Euston station via the pneumatic railway. ILLUSTRATED LONDON NEWS

journey at a rate, we are informed, of 20mph... a bell connected with an electric telegraph warns him that the attendant at the other end of the tube is about to thrust the carriage into the tube on its return journey.

"It has been pushed along... by the pressure of air thrown out by the wheel, but it has to be pulled back by suction; the valve of the suction-pipe, in the connection with the centre of the disc, is accordingly opened, and speedily we hear a hollow rumbling, and out shoots the carriage, ready once more for fresh bags."

The company sought to develop further lines within the capital, and construction began on a 3ft 8 ½ (please make a fraction) in-gauge line from Euston to Holborn in September 1863.

Its first 'trains' ran on October 10, 1865 after a demonstration in which chairman the 3rd Duke of Buckingham and Chandos travelled from Holborn to Euston in one of the capsules.

A third line from Holborn to Gresham Street via the General Post Office in St Martin's le Grand was started in 1865 and completed four years later.

Capsules from the General Post Office reached Newgate Street within 17 minutes, at speeds of up to 60mph.

The Post Office made several trials of the system, but found the insubstantial savings in time did not justify the cost. It was said the trucks containing the parcels continually got stuck in the tunnels. By 1874, the Post Office abandoned its use, and the company went into liquidation in 1875. Yes, the

Fig. 1.—The Pneumatic Dispatch—as first operated at Battersea Fields, London, in 1861.

Testing the London pneumatic railway at Battersea in 1861.

venture eventually failed financially, but it paved the way for the later Post Office underground railway.

In late-1921, an agreement was reached for the sale of what remained of the pneumatic railway to the Postmaster General for £7500, although it had long

since been anything near working order. The agreement was confirmed by the Post Office (Pneumatic Tubes) Act 1922.

Two of the original vehicles were preserved in 1930, one in the Museum of London and the other in the National Railway Museum at York.

RIGHT: A Wills cigarette card depiction of the first train on London's pneumatic postal railway.

BELOW: The Holborn end of the second pneumatic tube line on its opening day in 1865. ILLUSTRATED LONDON NEWS

WILLS'S CIGARETTES

INAUGURATION OF PNEUMATIC TUBE.

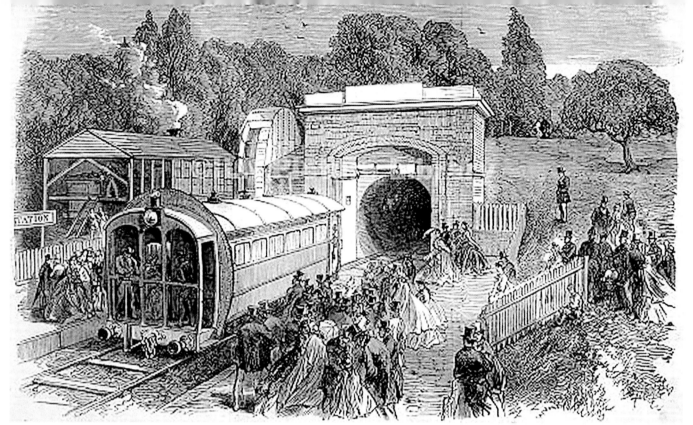

The short-lived Crystal Palace pneumatic railway, as sketched in 1864. ILLUSTRATED LONDON NEWS

BUILDING UP AIR BELOW CRYSTAL PALACE

Thomas Webster Rammell, who had built the railway for the London Pneumatic Despatch Company, used Brunel's 7ft¼in-broad gauge for a second but separate venture in Crystal Palace Park in 1864. The big difference was this one was designed to carry passengers.

The Crystal Palace line operated in much the same way as the postal one. A carriage equipped with a large collar of bristles was sucked along an airtight 10ft by 9ft tunnel. Power was provided by a 22ft-diameter fan, resembling a paddlewheel in an iron case. In turn, it was powered at 300rpm by a former steam locomotive mounted on a plinth, acting through leather belts. The bristle collar kept the tunnel 'partially airtight'. The tunnel was built in a 4ft-deep trench and ran for 600 yards between the Sydenham and Penge entrances to the park. The carriage could seat 35, and housed a sliding door at each end. It had to negotiate difficult bends along the line.

As the vehicle approached the lower terminus it was slowed by a short, uphill section of track and released propelling air pressure as it passed a grating open to the atmosphere. The only intervention required from the operator was the application of the brake.

On return journeys, the fan was reversed to create a vacuum to suck the carriage backwards, while the carriage used its brakes to come to a stop.

The coach probably travelled at around 25mph.

A newspaper account of the day called for steps to prevent any mechanical failure subjecting passengers to effects of vacuum like "frogs under a vacuum pump".

The line ran only between August and October 1864, with the fare being sixpence. Historians have speculated it may have been a testbed for a bigger pneumatic railway being planned to run between Waterloo station and pass under the River Thames upstream from Hungerford Bridge to the Whitehall end of Great Scotland Yard.

Construction began on the Waterloo & Whitehall Railway after it was authorised by a Parliament Act of 1865. However, the project fell foul of the financial collapse on 1866, and in September 1870, the Board of Trade declared it abandoned. The later Baker Street & Waterloo Railway, now London Underground's Bakerloo Line, followed a similar alignment,

Rumours circulated from the 1930s onwards that the site of the Crystal Palace railway is haunted. In 1978, a woman claimed to have found the tunnel and to have seen inside it an old railway carriage filled with skeletons in Victorian outfits. The story provided the inspiration for the novel Strange Air by fantasy writer Tom Brown.

THAMES RIVER, LONDON, PNEUMATIC DISPATCH TUBE.

The iron tube intended for use on the Waterloo & Whitehall Railway. ILLUSTRATED LONDON NEWS

FOSSIL FUELS OTHER THAN COAL

Other than the early electric locomotives we have seen, the Victorian railway age was built on the principle of coal-burning locomotives to produce steam. Even Brunel was limited by this factor: his South Devon atmospheric railway still burned coal, but at station engines rather than in the fireboxes of self-propelled vehicles.

With the dawn of the age of the motor car approaching, railway locomotive manufacturers began to look at internal combustion to replace steam. In 1894, Priestman Brothers of Hull built a basic and unsuccessful locomotive for use on the port's docks.

Two years later, Richard Hornsby & Sons Ltd in Lincolnshire built the first successful kerosene locomotive, *Lachesis*, for use on the 18in-gauge Woolwich Arsenal Railway. The firm built more such locomotives for the British Army between then and 1903.

The first commercially successful petrol locomotive was an 80hp petrol-mechanical, built by the Maudslay Motor Company in 1902 for London's Deptford cattle market.

Using a three-cylinder vertical petrol engine, it had a two-speed mechanical gearbox. FC Blake of Kew built another in January 1903 for the Richmond Main Sewerage Board.

From 1916, Simplex petrol locomotives, built by Motor-Rail Ltd of Bedford with 20-40 hp motors and four-wheel mechanical transmission, began to be used on 1ft 11⅝in-gauge (fraction please) trench railways on the Western Front.

Yet what about internal combustion traction used for passenger trains?

In the first years of the 20th century, many railway companies, principally the GWR, were developing steam railmotors, a concept designed to eradicate the need for a steam locomotive to run round its train at the end of a branch line. A steam bogie was built inside a carriage body, which could be operated

The first commercially successful internal combustion locomotive was built in 1902 by the Maudslay Motor Company for London's Deptford cattle market.

from their end – a self-propelled, all-in-one rail vehicle.

Drawing on experiments with tram technology, the Taff Vale Railway looked at the possibility of using battery-electric railcars and also a petrol-electric railcar for a lightly used rural route, but nothing came of it.

The GWR went so far as to produce a diagram of a petrol-engined railcar in February 1903, before any of the company's steam railmotors left the drawing board, and before the company began using petrol road buses on its route from Helston to Lizard Town in August that year, both as a feeder to their train services, and as a cheaper alternative to building new lines in sparsely populated rural areas.

Yet the North Eastern Railway went one better, and in terms of technological evolution, eclipsed everyone else. In May 1903, the NER unveiled a pair of 'autocars' – Nos. 3170 and 3171.

They were the first internal combustion-engined, self-propelled passenger-carrying rail vehicles in the world, and through them, the steam railmotor concept would evolve into the diesel railcar of the 1930s and beyond to the high-speed multiple units of today's railways.

They appeared three years before. In 1906, Rudolf Diesel, Adolf Klose and the steam and diesel engine

manufacturer Gebrüder Sulzer founded Diesel-Sulzer-Klose GmbH to manufacture diesel-powered locomotives. The world's first diesel-powered locomotive (a diesel-mechanical locomotive) was operated in the summer of 1912 on the Winterthur to Romanshorn railway in Switzerland, but was not a commercial success.

The NER's assistant chief mechanical engineer Vincent Raven was convinced about the advantages of electric traction, especially with regard to the hill-climbing ability of the early street trams he studied. Looking at those hills which his South Devon Railway would have to cross en route to Plymouth, Brunel would surely have bitten his hand off if offered an autocar or three!

Raven drew up a design for his autocars, incorporating electrical technology, but instead of picking up the current from overhead lines in tram fashion, he eliminated the need for expensive wires and masts by installing a power plant within the vehicle instead.

His autocar design was a steam railmotor minus the steam engine but with an 85hp Napier petrol engine powering a dynamo which supplied 550V to two 55hp electric motors, and drove the axles of the power bogie via gears.

The pair entered service in August 1904, one operating between West Hartlepool and Hartlepool stations in direct competition with electric street trams, and showed it could complete the journey in half the time of the rival service. The other replaced steam on the Scarborough to Filey route.

The autocars fell out of favour in the 1920s. One big criticism was their weight of 35 tons 15 cwt was high for the relatively low power output. Also, there was the old problem of two 'one-off' types of 'unusual' traction in a 'Big Four' company fleet dominated by steam. No. 3171 was withdrawn on May 31, 1930 and No. 3170 in April 1931. The body of the latter was sold to a North Yorkshire landowner and fitted with a tin roof and veranda, and became a holiday home at Keldholme, near Kirkbymoorside, on the North Yorkshire moors.

One of the two NER petrol-electric autocars waits at Scarborough station. NER 1903 ELECTRIC AUTOCAR TRUST

THE A-SHAPED STEAM MONORAIL

If Brunel could not convince the South Devon Railway directors to continue with atmospheric traction rather than steam locomotives, let alone the rest of the world, or that his broad gauge was superior to George Stephenson's 4ft 8½in, what chance did French engineer Charles Lartigue (1834-1907) have with his unique A-shaped monorail trestle and 'Siamese twins' engines?

Born in Toulouse in 1834, it was in his forties he saw camels in Algeria carrying heavy loads across the desert, balanced in panniers on their backs.

That inspired him to devise a completely new form of steam railway. Instead of locomotives and stock running on two rails fixed to the sleepers on the ground, why not have a single rail at waist height carried on trestles? The locomotives and rolling stock would then sit astride the track just like the camels' panniers.

By 1881, Lartigue had a 56-mile-long A-section monorail running across the Algerian desert, carrying esparto grass, with mules hauling the trains.

Lartique, who had taken a horse-drawn monorail system and the world's first elevated railway invented by Brunel contemporary Henry Robinson Palmer in 1821 several stages further, had a point with his project in the Sahara, where the shifting sands of the desert would have made a conventional railway unusable.

An A-shaped monorail might be a resounding success in the desert, but Lartigue overlooked the fact most of the rest of the world was not built on sand.

He demonstrated his system in London in 1886 in a vain bid to convince others it was better than the railways of the era.

However, an opportunity arose. Residents of North Kerry, demanding to be linked to the Irish railway network,

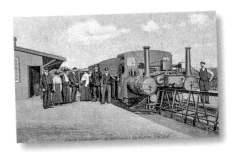

A hand-coloured postcard view of the Listowel & Ballybunion Railway in 1900.

arrived at Westminster, and it was suggested Lartigue's system could be tried over a nine-mile line between Listowel and Ballybunion, which wanted to become a major beach resort.

The railway cost £30,000 to build and opened on March 1, 1888, giving both towns instant international fame for being served by the world's first steam monorailway.

It was not a true monorail, because

THE MISSING LINK RETURNS

No. 3170 may have looked to the untrained eye just like any other redundant wooden-bodied railway coach from yesteryear, but there is far more to it than that.

In historical terms, as the bridge between steam and 'modern' traction, it may be considered as important in terms of the lineage of railway locomotive development as Stephenson's *Rocket* – and in 2018, it was set to carry passengers again.

Harrogate-based coach restorer Stephen Middleton had built up a reputation for restoring vintage vehicles which other groups shied away from as too difficult. In one instance, he even sold a prize collection of Hornby Dublo trains and horse dung to pay for carriage restoration.

In September 2003, Stephen bought the grounded body of No. 3170 from the

landowner, and moved it to join his other vehicles on the Embsay & Bolton Abbey Steam Railway. The following year, he drew together six experts from other heritage lines who shared his vision of restoring the autocar as near as possible to its rebuilt 1923 condition, and making it operational again.

They formed the North Eastern Railway 1903 Electric Autocar Trust and set about sourcing suitable components for the project, designing its rebuild, and most importantly, fundraising to make it happen. A suitable underframe was secured from the LNER Coach Association. Plans were drawn up to have them re-engineered to take a new engine, generator, traction motors and control equipment.

Despite the vehicle's paramount importance to world transport history, modern regulations would not allow the

use of an old petrol engine, so a diesel alternative, while not authentic, was sourced as a second-best option.

A suitable motor bogie was identified, from a Southern Region Class 416 (2EPB) EMU, and brought to Embsay. The reasoning behind the choice of a Class 416 bogie and its motors is the fact they are compatible with modern diesel generators and control equipment. However, the bogie received a major overhaul in 2003 and has seen little use since.

The project deservedly attracted money from the Heritage Lottery Fund, which gave a grant of £465,000, with additional finance from the Preservation of Industrial and Scientific Material (PRISM) Fund, the Ken Hoole Trust, plus members and supporters.

Although the original underframe had three petrol engines powering a generator, this one has a £40,000 350hp Darlington-built Cummins QSL9 diesel engine, making it appropriate for regular use on heritage railways.

The LNER had considered extending the life of the autocar by fitting a diesel engine. No. 3170's engine is the first UK-built diesel electric engine since the Class 60s.

History was made on the Great Central Railway with the first test runs of the chassis of No. 3170 in preservation, between Loughborough and Quorn & Woodhouse, on March 17, 2016.

Following testing, the underframe returned to Embsay, where the body is ready to fit. A suitable trailer coach has also been restored at Embsay.

The autocar made its passenger-carrying comeback on the Embsay line in autumn 2018.

A star is reborn: NER petrol-electric autocar No. 3170 at Embsay. NER 1903 ELECTRIC AUTOCAR TRUST

on each side of the trestle lay another rail, which carried unpowered stabilising wheels fitted to all the engines and wagons to prevent them from overbalancing.

In October 1887, Leeds engine builder Hunslet supplied three engines to the line, designed by fabled articulated locomotive engineer Anatole Mallet. They were 0-6-0s – or rather, 0-3-0s. Looking like steam Siamese twins, they were specially built with two boilers in order to balance on the track, and therefore needed two fireboxes, one of which had to be stoked by the driver, the other in the time-honoured way by the fireman. It was said the engines could haul a load of 240 tons at 30mph.

They also had powered tenders to give extra power when climbing gradients. The tender wheels were driven by two cylinders via spur gears, and a pair of small chimneys were fitted to each tender to discharge the steam from these cylinders.

Therefore, the Listowel & Ballybunion locomotives had a wheel arrangement of 0-3-0 + 0-2-0. However, the boilers could not generate enough steam to run the tender engines as well, and they were never used.

As well as passengers, the trains carried freight, cattle, plus sand from the beaches to use as fertiliser. Golfers travelled over the line to the then-new course at Ballybunion, which eventually became regarded as one of the best in the world.

However, freight loads had to be evenly balanced. If a farmer sent a cow to market via monorail, he would have to send two calves to balance it. They would travel back on opposite sides of the same freight wagon, thereby balancing each other. Similarly, passengers could not pass from one side of a carriage to another while the train was running.

Also, it was impossible to build level crossings. When a road was encountered, a double-sided

The replica steam outline Listowel & Ballybunion locomotive encounters one of the points. The train travels at 15mph while on the main line, about the same speed as the originals.

drawbridge had to be provided, with an attendant to operate it.

Where farmers' tracks crossed the line, level crossings took the form of a swivelling turntable, locked before and after use, with the farmer given a key.

Worse still, traditional railway points were out of the question, so more trestle-mounted turntables were needed to access sidings and passing loops.

Speaking plainly, the monorail design was workable, but ludicrous by comparison with conventional railways. Unlike the atmospheric railway he saw elsewhere in Ireland, I don't think for a minute Brunel would have taken the Lartigue system seriously.

Remarkably, unlike many other rural railways of the day, the railway just about managed to break even, and ran for 36 years.

Its closure came as a result of damage during the Irish Civil War of 1922/23. The line closed in 1924 and everything was scrapped apart from a short section of track.

The Kerry line was not unique. After it opened, an 11-mile 'Lartigue line' was built to serve Panissières in the Loire

region of France, with two locomotives, named Feurs and Panissières. Tests in 1895/96 proved less than satisfactory, and the line was finally sold for scrap in 1902.

Lartigue died in 1907. The last Lartigue monorail was opened by the Sierra Salt Corporation in California's Mojave Desert in the mid-1920s. It worked well for two years, only for the mine to close.

After a Lartigue Restoration Committee was established in the 1990s to celebrate the heritage of the bizarre line, English locomotive builder Alan Keef Ltd of Ross-on-Wye was asked to build a replica locomotive, but for ease of operation, to use a diesel motor. Keef was also contracted to construct a pair of third-class carriages.

In 2003, a 1000-metre section of Lartigue monorail on the trackbed of the former line was opened, complete with three points, a pair of turntables and three platforms representing Listowel, Lisselton and Ballybunion.

The site of the original Lartigue station is preserved in a park next to the new monorail.

An original Lartigue train arriving at Ballybunion.

TOWARDS THE SPACE AGE: HOVER RAIL!

Just as Brunel believed he had found the traction of the future in the atmospheric section of the Dalkey & Kingstown Railway, so the invention of the hovercraft in the Fifties set like minds thinking – could the principle be applied to a new form of railway?

With the space race between the United States and the Soviet Union grabbing the imagination, with rockets pointing the way to the moon and maybe beyond, it seemed new futuristic forms

of everyday transport would be just around the corner.

Aero and marine engineering company and flying boat builder Saunders-Roe Limited, based at Columbine Works, in East Cowes, on the Isle of Wight, demonstrated the Saunders-Roe Nautical 1 (SR-N1) on June 11, 1959. It was the first hovercraft built to inventor Christopher Cockerell's design. Two weeks later it crossed the English Channel from Calais to Dover, paving the

way for a series of similar air-cushioned sea craft. Yet if it worked on sea, why not on land – and could it be adapted to create a new form of railway?

Several attempts were made to adopt air-cushion technology for use in fixed-track systems, taking advantage of lower frictional forces to produce high speeds. In France, Aérotrain, an experimental high-speed hovertrain, was operated between 1965 and 1977. It ended up being scrapped because of lack of

A view from the cab of prototype hovertrain RTV31 on its test track at Earith, near Cambridge, in 1972.

LEFT: Britain's only hovertrain, RTV31, is preserved at the entrance to Railworld. ROBIN JONES

funding, and the French government adopted the alternative TGV as its high-speed rail solution.

Here in England, four miles of a planned 20-mile test track between the Old Bedford River and the smaller Counter Drain in the Cambridgeshire fens was built by Tracked Hovercraft Ltd at Earith, as far as Sutton-in-the-Isle. The track was around 6ft above the ground, and it was expected the test rain would reach 300mph.

The hovertrain concept had originated with English engineer Professor Eric

Laithwaite (June 14, 1921-November 27, 1997) of Imperial College London, who, in the late Forties, demonstrated the first full-size working model of a linear induction motor.

His ideas were harnessed for Research Test Vehicle 31, or RTV31, the prototype for a hovercraft rail system at Earith. The vehicle used linear magnetic motors for forward motion, and a cushion of air, powered from giant fans to lift itself off the track, was built for the tests.

From a standing start, RTV31 reached

This building at Earith in Cambridgeshire is the original hangar used for the Tracked Hovercraft project. The outline of the original opening for RVT31 can be seen as the trapezoidal area on the main building. LEE DALTON

LEFT: A project that never got as close to reality as Brunel's atmospheric railway: a scale model of the stalled British hovertrain. It was hoped the hovertrain would take passengers from London to Glasgow in little more than two hours at speeds of up to 300mph. It would have revolutionised long-distance travel and therefore consigned conventional trains to the history books – but it never happened.

104mph over a mile on February 7, 1973, echoing the impressive speeds obtained by Brunel's atmospheric railway.

Yet only a week after this run, funding for the project was cancelled by the Ted Heath Government's Aerospace Minister Michael Heseltine. The system was considered to be too expensive for commercial use.

The Government, which had stumped up more than £5million in funding for the hovertrain project, decided to focus on the almost equally ill-fated Advanced Passenger Train tilting train project. So the hovertrain, along with all its promise and hubris, was quickly forgotten.

The late MP Airey Neave and others accused Heseltine of misleading the House of Commons by stating the Government was still considering backing for the hovertrain project, despite the fact the Cabinet had already decided otherwise.

In 1975, little more than five years after construction started, the test track was demolished and the project was unceremoniously mothballed.

RTV 31 ended up at Cranfield University where it was kept in the open for more than 20 years. In 1996 it was donated to Railword, Peterborough's railway heritage museum, which sits alongside the city's Nene Valley Railway station. There, RYV31 was restored and set up as a main display at the entrance, and can be seen from passing trains on the East Coast Main Line as one of the great might-have-beens, just like Brunel's South Devon Railway.

The Birmingham International Airport pioneer maglev train in operation. GCMALTA*

FLOATING ON AIR: THAT MAGNETIC ATTRACTION!

In parallel with his tracked hovercraft rail system, Eric Laithwaite was developing another form of hovertrain, based around magnetic levitation. It became known as maglev.

A wheel-less maglev train uses powerful electro-magnets to lift itself off its track, whereas RTV31 used a cushion of air.

A pair of maglev vehicles entered commercial service in Britain on August 16, 1984, on a 1969ft elevated line linking the then-new Birmingham International Airport terminal to Birmingham International railway station. It was the first commercial maglev service in the world.

A maglev car from the Birmingham line inside the National Railway Museum at York. ROBIN JONES

The driverless cars 'flew' at a height of 15mm and each carried up to 40 passengers with their luggage.

The linear motor was naturally suited to use with maglev systems as well as monorails. In the early Seventies, Laithwaite had discovered a new arrangement of magnets, the magnetic river, that allowed a single linear motor to produce both lift and forward thrust, allowing a maglev system to be built with a single set of magnets. Working at the British Rail Research Division in Derby, along with teams at several civil engineering firms, the 'transverse-flux' system was developed into a working system.

The concept, however, was far from new. Early US patents for a linear motor-propelled train were awarded to German inventor Alfred Zehden in 1905 and 1907. A series of German patents for magnetic levitation trains propelled by linear motors were awarded to Hermann Kemper from 1937-41, and an early maglev train was described in a US patent of 1959 awarded to G R Polgreen.

Transrapid 05 was the first maglev train with long-stator propulsion licensed for passenger transportation. In 1979, a 2979ft track was opened in Hamburg for the first International Transportation Exhibition. Interest in this new novel form of alternative transportation was such that operations were extended three months after the exhibition finished, having carried more than 50,000 passengers. It was reassembled in Kassel in 1980.

The initial feasibility studies for a link from Birmingham's airport to the railway station and adjoining National Exhibition Centre were started in 1979 by the owners of the airport at that time, West Midlands County Council.

The selected solution was based on the experimental work at Derby.

Contracts were awarded in 1981 to a consortium involving GEC, Balfour Beatty, Brush Electrical Machines and Metropolitan Cammell under the banner of People Mover Group, along with John Laing plc.

The carriages were manufactured by Metropolitan Cammell Carriage & Wagon Company Metropolitan Cammell, builder of railway coaches since 1863, at its Washwood Heath plant in Birmingham.

The aeroport line operated for many years, but parts of its electrical systems became obsolete, and it became increasingly difficult to source spare parts. There were numerous breakdowns, leaving passengers stranded mid-line.

I have fond personal memories of Birmingham's maglev. Firstly, when I worked as a journalist there, I had a small but profitable sideline tipping off local radio stations every time maglev broke down, leaving passengers stranded in mid-journey, but giving me a handy monthly cheque coming through the letterbox. At one stage it was happening two or three times a week, so I was quids in – maybe a rare example of someone making a profit from maglev.

Then when my fiancé and I were looking for a venue for our wedding reception in 1988, we decided a spacious plush conference suite at the airport fitted the bill better than everywhere else. The doors to the airport's maglev station were immediately opposite those of the suite, and once some of the guests realised, they queued up to take trips on it!

The system closed in July 1995 after an investigation concluded the cost of reinstating and maintaining the maglev to be too high. Initially, the cars for the maglev were stored by the airport owners, Birmingham International Airport Ltd, on the airport site.

Maglev was eventually replaced by the AirRail Link people-mover, cabled-hauled system, using the same concrete guideway.

Work on a replacement project began on March 30, 2001 and was completed on March 7, 2003 with the first day of public operation. The project contract cost £11 million.

The current AirRail Link is a cable-propelled, double shuttle system. It is built on top of the previous maglev guideway, slightly shortened by an extension of the railway station concourse to accommodate a low-level bus station. It has two independent rope-hauled parallel tracks and a two-car passenger unit operating on each track.

The second commercial maglev operation was an elevated mile-long line operating in Berlin from 1989-91. The line was built to fill a gap in the public transport network created by the construction of the Berlin Wall, and was rendered redundant by the reunification of Berlin when the wall came down.

While maglev failed to take off in the UK long term, the concept has been successfully embraced by other countries.

In Japan, the development of the JR-Maglev by Japan Railways Group began in 1969 and in 2003, it reached a speed of nearly 344mph in tests.

The Central Japan Railway Company intends to start a commercial maglev service between Tokyo and Nagoya in 2025.

The world's first commercial

Maglev replacement AirRail Link connects Birmingham International Airport and railway station with a pair of cable-driven people movers.

automated urban maglev system, a 5½-mile line between Tobu and Kyuryo, in Aichi, in March 2005, has a top speed of 62 mph. At a cost $1.2 billion, German firm Transrapid built the world's first operational high-speed conventional maglev railway, the 18¾-mile Shanghai maglev Train or Shanghai Transrapid, serving Pudong International Airport. The first services ran in 2002 and a speed of 311mph has been recorded.

The Shanghai maglev train became the third commercially operated magnetic levitation line in history, and the world's fastest commercial high-speed electric train, but has been said to have run up huge operating losses.

The development of the original maglev design is still continuing in earnest in the USA, Germany and Far East and USA, with more prototype systems being produced.

Despite the Birmingham failure,

maglev was suggested for a new high-speed trunk railway linking London to Scotland, but in 2010 the Labour Government announced that traditional railway technology would be used instead.

Again, what would Brunel have done if the technology had been available in his day? I do not think he would have hesitated to adopt it, but he had to settle for a vacuum pipe instead.

Eventually, Eric Laithwaite's RTV31 and maglev would be united. At Railworld, the aforementioned railway museum in Peterborough, RTV31 takes pride of place astride a saved section of the concrete test track at the entrance.

Inside, placed firmly in a flower bed with no chance of levitation, sits a maglev car from the Birmingham scheme. A sister vehicle is inside the Great Hall of the National Railway Museum at York, while another was sold for charity on eBay to an enthusiast.

A maglev train leaving Pudong International Airport in Shanghai.

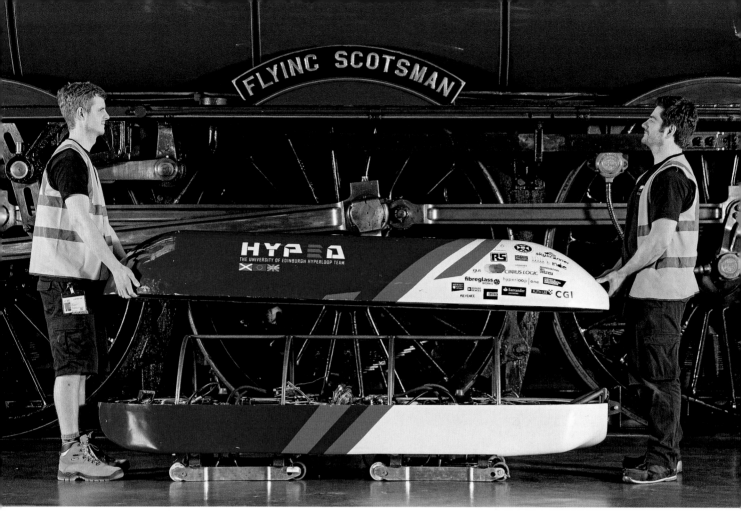

Britain's first prototype Hyperloop pod demonstrated at the National Railway Museum in York. JODY HARTLEY/NRM

NEXT STOP: THE HYPERLOOP

As we have seen, ever since the dawn of railways, inventors have been vying to find a futuristic method of transport that goes one better than the last.

Had the right materials been available to Isambard Brunel when he oversaw the building of the South Devon atmospheric railway, I have little doubt it would have been a success and would have paved the way (even with a vacuum pipe in the middle of that way!) for other railways to have followed. With the impressive speeds his atmospheric trains clocked up between Exeter and Newton Abbot, who knows what direction the evolution of railways might have taken?

However, following on from maglev is the Hyperloop, which, on paper at least, would make Brunel's atmospheric railway look like a tortoise on tranquillisers.

Hyperloop is a new form of transport currently in development by a number of companies, which could see passengers travelling at more than 700mph in floating pods inside low-pressure tubes or tunnels from which most of the air has been removed to reduce friction.

Rather than using wheels like a conventional train, the pods float on air skis or again, use magnetic levitation to reduce friction.

The concept of using low pressure or vacuum tubes as a transport system dates back to the pre-Brunel work of George Medhurst, which in turn

influenced the postal lines built by the London Pneumatic Despatch Company and the short-lived passenger-carrying Crystal Palace version.

Today, it is South African-born entrepreneur Elon Musk who is driving the Hyperloop concept forward.

Musk, who in February 2018 had a net worth of $20.8billion, and was listed by Forbes as the 53rd-richest person in the world, published his Hyperloop Alpha paper in August 2013, setting out the cost and benefits of such a project, which would be ideal for a system linking cities 900 miles apart.

In the paper, Musk argued the case for a Hyperloop service between Los Angeles and San Francisco, one which would be cheaper and faster than a proposed high-speed rail link.

He said: "How would you like something that can never crash, is immune to weather, goes three or four times faster than the bullet train... goes an average speed of twice what an aircraft would do?

"You would go from downtown LA to downtown San Francisco in under 30 minutes. It would cost you much less than an air ticket and any other mode of transport.

"I think we could actually make it self-powering if you put solar panels on it; you generate more power than you would consume in the system."

The pressure of air inside the Hyperloop tube is about one-sixth the pressure of the atmosphere on

Mars, in the version of the technology espoused by Musk. Several companies are now reportedly racing to develop Hyperloop technology, and routes under consideration include New York to Washington DC, Kansas City to St Louis, Pune to Mumbai and Bratislava to Brno.

However, at the moment, the Hyperloop seems little more than a series of bold claims and a basic test track in the Nevada desert – echoing somewhat Britain's monorail test track at Earith in Cambridgeshire in 1973.

On April 26, 2018, the National Railway Museum in York displayed Britain's first Hyperloop prototype, which has been developed by students at the University of Edinburgh and which, in theory, travelling inside near-vacuum tubes at speeds of up to 650mph, could cut York to London journey times to just 20 minutes.

The Hyperloop pod was displayed in the museum's Great Hall alongside the world's most famous steam locomotive, LNER A3 Pacific No. 60103 *Flying Scotsman*, and Class 88 electro-diesel No. 88002 *Prometheus*.

The university team has competed in several international Hyperloop competitions and won a number of prestigious awards. The prototype will be going on public display at the museum later in the year.

The April 26 event highlighted the museum's commitment to tell the story of the current and future of railway innovation, as well as more than 200

National Railway Museum director Judith McNicol with *Flying Scotsman*, Class 88 electro-diesel *Prometheus* and the prototype Hyperloop pod. JODY HARTLEY/NRM

years of history, and to inspire and develop the engineers of the future, who may well include a 21st-century Isambard.

Museum director Judith McNicol said: "Today's event offers an exciting glimpse of what could be around the corner in terms of high-speed passenger transport, and is a celebration of the past, present and future of the railways."

Who knows? Maybe Brunel got it just slightly wrong – the carriages should not have been pulled along by the vacuum pipe, but should have been inside the pipe itself!

So long a nickname for London Undergound, future generations may have a new use for the term 'The Tube'.

AND THE LATEST ARRIVAL

On July 28, 2018, the modern-day Great Western Railway's newest train type crosses the Dawlish sea wall for the first time. The 12.10pm arrival at Paignton from Paddington marked the first Intercity Express Train to travel to the seaside town. The nine-carriage Class 800 unit No. 800309 became the first Intercity Express Train to travel from London beyond Exeter in passenger service, marking another milestone in the roll out of the new fleet.

Torbay MP Kevin Foster said: "The arrival of GWR's new Intercity Express Trains into our bay is a great moment not just for the passengers who will use them, but our region as a whole as these trains speed to the South West for the first time.

"These sleek new trains will replace the current fleet built in the 1970s, improving journey times, comfort and reliability."

"One hundred and seventy years after Brunel built the GWR his legacy lives on as these iconic trains use his iconic coastal railway."

Dawlish councillor Rosalind Prowse said: "This is welcome news. I am aware of the importance of the railway and without it the economy of the South West would suffer.

"With the large amount of development in Devon and Cornwall it is necessary to have an updated service carrying us forward into the 21st century.

"We are here today because of IK Brunel, and it is a pleasure to think we continue with his vision."

Class 800 unit No. 800309, seen at Paignton on July 28, 2018. That day became an example of the newest type to run over Dawlish sea wall, the route built for revolutionary but short-lived atmospheric trains. GWR

Chapter 7

SON OF THE FATHER!

George Stephenson may have started out as illiterate, but became known in historical terms as the Father of the Railways. His only son Robert received a half-decent education – and there are those who regard him as the greatest engineer of the 19th century.

Robert Stephenson first attended a village school in Long Benton, where he was taught by Thomas Rutter. On his way to school, he would carry picks to the village smithy at Long Benton to be sharpened. While George had received little formal education, he was determined that his son would not lose out in the same way, and so sent Robert at the age of 11 to be taught by John Bruce at the Percy Street Academy in Newcastle. Most of the children came from middle-class families, and it was while he was at the academy that Robert lost most of his Northumberland accent.

Robert Stephenson: One of the greatest railway and bridge builders.

The original entrance to the London & Birmingham Railway's London terminus at Euston – the first inter-city railway terminal in London, planned by George and Robert Stephenson. The original station was designed by Philip Hardwick and built by William Cubitt. The site was chosen in 1831 by George and Robert in an area that was mostly farmland at the edge of the expanding city. The station was named after Euston Hall in Suffolk, the ancestral home of the Dukes of Grafton, the main landowners in the area. The main entrance portico, known as the Euston Arch, was also designed by Hardwick, and was designed to symbolise the arrival of a major new transport system as well as being seen as 'the gateway to the north'. It stood 72ft high, supported four 44ft 2in hollow Doric propylaeum columns, and was completed in May 1838. The structure was controversially demolished in the 1960s.

Robert walked the 10 miles to the academy each day, but was prone to catching colds. His father feared he would contract tuberculosis so he bought him a donkey to speed up the journey.

Robert became a member of the Newcastle Literary and Philosophical Society which loaned him books for him and his father to read. At home in the evening, the pair would work together on designs for steam engines.

He left school in 1819 and became apprenticed to mining engineer Nicholas Wood, the manager of Killingworth Colliery. He seized the chance and became determined to progress in the field.

Robert could not afford to buy a mining compass, so he made one himself, and later used it to survey High Level Bridge in Newcastle.

However, Robert began showing signs of tuberculosis while he was working down the mine. Wood agreed to release Robert so he could help his father survey the Stockton & Darlington Railway, during which time George was persuaded his son should undergo a short university academic year. It goes without saying that a formal education would help elevate him to a par with the likes of Isambard Brunel at an early age.

Robert helped William James to

Next off the Robert Stephenson & Co production line after *Rocket* was four-wheeled locomotive *Invicta*, the 20th to be built by the company. It was designed for the Canterbury & Whitstable Railway – which opened four months before the Liverpool & Manchester Railway. In 1834, the world's first season ticket was issued on the Canterbury & Whitstable, nicknamed the 'Crab & Winkle Line'. Redundant by 1839, *Invicta* was donated to Canterbury City Corporation as a museum artefact, and became the world's first preserved locomotive. It is pictured in Canterbury Heritage Museum in December 2010. ROBIN JONES

The Camden Town engine house as sketched in 1838.

LEFT: A train of third class carriages await departure from Euston in 1837.

carry out the original survey of the Liverpool & Manchester Railway in 1822, and then he attended classes in Natural Philosophy, Natural History and Chemistry at Edinburgh University.

The second Stockton & Darlington Railway Act received Royal Assent on May 23, 1823, with permission to use locomotives on it. A month later, both Stephenson's and the line's promoter Edward Pease opened a locomotive building firm – Robert Stephenson and Company in Forth Street, Newcastle – to supply engines.

While George supervised the building of the railway, Robert was placed in charge of the works on a £200-a-year salary. He also surveyed the line's Hagger Leases freight branch, which served local collieries.

Parliament required a new Act for the line, after which it ordered two steam locomotives and two stationary engines from the firm on September 16, 1824. However, at that time, Robert was absent. He had taken a three-year contract with the Colombian Mining Association, which had embarked on a venture to reopen gold and silver mines in South America.

The association ordered steam engines from the company, and one of his partners, Thomas Richardson, also a partner in the venture, suggested Robert should go, and he agreed. He visited Cornish mines and took Spanish lessons to prepare himself, and set sail from Liverpool to Colombia on June 18, 1824.

The great viaduct and embankment built for the London & Birmingham Railway at Watford.

The longest embankment on the London & Birmingham Railway spanned the valley of the River Great Ouse. One and a half miles long, it included the imposing six-arch, 46ft-high Wolverton Viaduct to the north of the station yard. There were many problems encountered during construction, especially landslips on the nearby embankment. They can still be seen just south of the viaduct and are portrayed here by John Cooke Bourne.

It has been suggested the real reason Robert left was because he wanted to be his own man, not guided by his father.

It was not a happy time for Robert in Colombia. He failed to get plans for a railway and pier at La Guayra in Venezuela off the ground, and when he reached the Colombian mines, he found they were largely worked by often-drunk Cornish miners, who would not accept him because he was not from the Duchy.

His contract ended on July 16, 1827, and he later experienced a series of adventures. These included a meeting with steam locomotive engineer Richard Trevithick, who had been looking for gold and silver in the mines of Peru and Costa Rica; a shipwreck en route to New York, in which he lost his money and luggage; and a 500-mile walk with four fellow English expatriates to Montreal via the Niagara Falls so he could see something of North America.

He finally arrived back in Liverpool in November 1827, and briefly stayed with his father, who by then was chief engineer of the Liverpool & Manchester Railway.

He then returned to work at Robert Stephenson & Co, making improvements to his father's steam engine designs and building new ones, while also surveying routes for other railways.

On June 17, 1829, he married an old friend, Frances (Fanny) Sanderson, in London. In October that year, the Rainhill Trials (Chapter 2) were held,

and Robert worked extensively on *Rocket*, his father's entrant. It has been said the son had the greater input into the locomotive.

The Liverpool & Manchester Railway bought *Rocket* and ordered four similar locomotives from Robert Stephenson & Co before the end of October. Four more similar locomotives followed, before *Planet* was delivered on October 4, 1830, with cylinders placed horizontally under the boiler, the next stage in evolution from *Rocket*.

The firm supplied *John Bull*, a *Planet*-type locomotive, to the US and became the first movement by steam in New Jersey when it ran on the Camden and Amboy Railroad in 1831. By then the firm was receiving so many orders for locomotives that Robert opted to open another one, on the doorstep of the Liverpool & Manchester and associated railways. He became a partner in the Vulcan Foundry, which built engines

The London & Birmingham Railway's coat of arms

A London & Birmingham Railway train approaches the tunnel at Leighton Buzzard.

Artist John Cooke Bourne, who as we saw earlier sketched so much of Isambard Brunel's Great Western Railway while it was under construction, recorded the excavation of the London & Birmingham Railway's Tring Cutting. As at Sonning Cutting, the work was carried out by navvies using just picks and shovels.

The surviving Grade I-listed entrance building at Birmingham's Curzon Street station was designed by Philip Hardwick. Built in 1838, it is the world's oldest surviving piece of monumental railway architecture. A commemorative plaque reads: 'This plaque commemorates the 150th anniversary of the arrival of the first London to Birmingham train at this station on Monday, September 17 1838'. ROBIN JONES

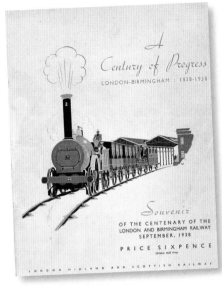

One of Edmund Bury's 0-4-0s built for the London & Birmingham Railway is depicted on the cover of a centenary booklet produced by the LMS in 1928. Wolverton was one of the railway's great workshops, a midway point between England's first and second cities, and in 1836, seasoned engineer Bury became the line's locomotive works superintendent. His designs had previously been criticised by George Stephenson when he had tried to get the Liverpool & Manchester Railway to build them. However, by 1841, when there were 88 of his four-wheelers supplied by his own Liverpool company in service on the London & Birmingham, it became clear they were too small for the task, and became all but obsolete. In 1845, he began building more powerful six-wheelers at Wolverton.

at Newton-le-Willows.

Back home, Robert oversaw the construction of the Canterbury & Whitstable Railway, which opened on May 3, 1830 with *Invicta*, a locomotive similar to *Rocket*, and the next off the Robert Stephenson & Co production line. Robert was also appointed as engineer of the Bolton & Leigh and Warrington & Newton railways, both branches of the Liverpool & Manchester, and the Leicester & Swannington Railway.

George Stephenson & Son was a separate company, formed in 1824, but with the same directors as Robert Stephenson & Co. The company's aim was to survey and build new lines.

On September 18, 1830, the company was given the contract to survey the route for the London & Birmingham Railway.

This time around, Robert did most of the work and stood as the engineering authority when a bill was presented to Parliament in 1832. Rejected by the Lords after a public campaign and another survey by Robert, the necessary Act was obtained on May 6, 1833, and

approval for the 112-mile line from Camden to London was given. At the age of 29, it was Robert who signed the contract on September 20. Needless to say, the line was built to the Stephenson gauge of 4ft 8½in.

As engineer of the next inter-city line, Robert was paid an annual salary of £1,500, plus £200 expenses.

Primrose Hill Tunnel, Wolverton embankment, and Kilsby Tunnel were all significant engineering feats, but to take the railway further into London, an incline with a slope between 1-in-75

The train shed at Birmingham Curzon Street in 1838.

RIGHT: Robert Stephenson & Co's Forth Street Works in Newcastle-upon-Tyne became suppliers of steam locomotives to the world.

J S Bourne's sketch of the interior of 2400-yard Kilsby Tunnel and its great air shaft. The tunnel was considered to be the most challenging – and expensive – engineering feat on the whole of the London & Birmingham Railway. Note the archaic use of iron blocks to hold the rails, as opposed to wooden sleepers. Robert Stephenson followed his father's practice of using this method of track work, but while it was fine for horse-drawn tramways, its use for a major trunk railway using heavy steam locomotives was widely criticised and led to track spreading. The line's original malleable iron rails were finally replaced in 1857.

and 1-in-66 was at first worked by a stationary engine at Camden, taking trains into Euston station, to comply with the terms of the enabling Act.

In reality, locomotives worked the section from when it opened on July 20, 1837, and whenever the stationary engine broke down, and entirely from July 15, 1844, Robert's friend Charles Wheatstone installed the first electric telegraph between Euston square and Camden Town stations in autumn 1837.

Building the line had taken four years

and three months, and cost more than double its £2.4million budget.

The first trains ran between London and Birmingham on June 24, 1838, with the line officially opened on September 15, later that year.

It has been said Robert Stephenson's most original contribution to civil engineering when building this line was his technique of constructing skew bridges, by which arch stone was formed and used like the thread of a screw.

While working for the London & Birmingham, Robert had agreed not to undertake any other engineering project, but could act as consultant on them. In 1835, George and Robert advised King Leopold of Belgium on that country's state railway, which opened between Brussels and Ghent in 1837.

Robert's services were so much in demand, he opened offices in Duke Street and then in Great George Street, Westminster, eventually occupying a building next door to the Institution of Civil Engineers, of which he had become a member. The office was also shared by George.

ANOTHER PEAK OF SUCCESS

Just as Isambard Brunel added more and more new railways to his design and engineering portfolio over and above his Great Western Railway, so the Stephenson father-and-son combination expanded the technological empire.

The Stanhope and Tyne Railroad Company was formed on April 20, 1832 as a partnership to build a railway between the lime kilns at Lanehead Farmhouse and the coal mines at Consett in County Durham. The partners had decided to build a railway instead of upgrading the Pontop Waggonway, and commissioned Robert as surveyor and consulting engineer. Building started at Stanhope in July 1832.

The Stanhope & Tyne Railway was considered challenging and ground-breaking at the time, but was soon outmoded by developments in steam technology.

The moorland in the west of the Durham coalfield rises to a ridge between 800-900ft above sea level, on which were the pit heads of some of the biggest collieries. To avoid the expense of major engineering works, rope haulage was widely used, allowing railways to be built more directly (often with very steep gradients) than would have been possible with horse or steam locomotive adhesion working.

Its 1474ft summit at Parkhead was the highest railway summit in England and Wales, apart from Snowdon.

A total of 14 miles of the route between Stanhope and Annfield was worked by stationary winding engines and horses, and the other three-quarters of a mile by gravity.

The first locomotive arrived in South Shields on May 1, 1834, and the Stanhope-Annfield section opened a fortnight later.

At Hownes Gill, an 800ft-wide and 160ft-deep valley 10 miles from Stanhope, it was decided a viaduct

Kilingworth Colliery as seen in the 1850s.

would be too expensive, so a cost-effective method was devised, with 7ft-gauge tracks laid on each face of the ravine, with gradients of 1-in-2.5 on the western side and 1-in-3 on the eastern.

A special cradle or truck was built for each track to carry standard gauge wagons, which having reached the bottom, were then transferred to the other cradle to be hauled up the other side. A small stationary engine situated at the bottom provided the power to haul the ropes.

The eastern section of the line involved no major engineering works and was officially opened on September 10, 1834. Every form of motive power then available – horses and locomotives, stationary engines and self-acting inclines – was used over various sections.

In 1835, the railway began to carry passengers, at first in coal wagons without payment and then in open carriages attached to the coal trains.

By the end of 1840 the company was bankrupt and the line from Stanhope to Carrhouse, near Consett, was closed.

Facing personal bankruptcy, Robert Stephenson himself tackled the company's difficulties. The proprietors agreed to promote a new statutory company to take over the property and debts, transferring the eastern part of the railway to a new Pontop & South Shields Railway Company, incorporated by an Act of Parliament on May 23, 1842, which raised capital to pay off the debts.

The Derwent Iron Company bought the remaining section between Stanhope and Consett along with the Stanhope limestone quarries, and drew up plans for a new railway from Waskerley to meet the Stockton & Darlington Railway at Crook, which opened on May 16, 1845.

The Stockton & Darlington took possession of both lines in January 1845, and over the next 18 years replaced all but one of the inclines.

Meanwhile, the Pontop & South Shields Railway was taken over on January 1, 1847, by the York & Newcastle Railway, which in July 1854 became part the North Eastern Railway.

After the Stockton & Darlington became part of the NER in 1863, the whole of the original Stanhope & Tyne line was once more under single ownership.

The line north of Tow Law to Blackhill was closed to passengers in May 1939. The entire Stanhope & Tyne route closed on May 1, 1969, because of the decline in stone traffic.

A BREAK IN GAUGE!
It might be expected the Stephensons would adhere to 'their' gauge of 4ft 8½in once it had proved such a dazzling success. Not so on the London & Blackwall Railway, which appointed Robert as engineer.

Originally called the Commercial Railway, the London & Blackwall Railway in east London, ran from Minories to Blackwall via Stepney, with a branch line to the Isle of Dogs, connecting central London to many of London's docks.

The engineer of the line was intended to be John Rennie, but the project's City financiers favoured Robert Stephenson, believing they would also benefit from the knowledge and wisdom of his respected father George.

Because of the Act, Robert Stephenson had to follow Rennie's route and use the obscure track gauge of 5ft½in, but he was free to choose his own method of propulsion. Drawing on his experience with the Camden Incline on the London & Birmingham Railway he decided upon cable haulage from stationary steam engines.

The railway was on brick arches as far as the West India Docks, and then on an embankment before entering a shallow cutting near the Blackwall terminus at Brunswick Wharf. The station there had an iron-roofed shed, and offices designed in an Italianate style by William Tite.

The line opened on July 6, 1840, and the company changed its name to the London & Blackwall Railway on completion of an extension to Fenchurch Street, just within the City boundary, in 1841.

YET MORE RAILWAYS

George and Robert Stephenson were appointed as engineers of the 72-mile North Midland Railway, which was designed to link Derby with the York & North Midland Railway at Normanton in Wakefield and the Manchester & Leeds Railway, and form part of a trunk route from London and the south of England to the industrial north.

The standard gauge line received parliamentary assent in 1836, and was completed to Masborough, near Rotherham, where it met the Sheffield & Rotherham Railway, on May 11, 1840, and on to Leeds on July 1.

At Derby, it linked to the Birmingham & Derby Junction Railway and the Midland Counties Railway at what became known as the Tri Junct station. In 1844, the three companies merged to form the Midland Railway.

George plotted a course for the line following river valleys from Derby to Leeds, with minimal gradients and large radii curves. It was one of a new kind of railway, one which aimed to improve passenger travel between cities, rather than carry heavy freight, including coal and minerals, from mines and quarries. However, it still needed 200 bridges, including the massive Calder and Chevet viaducts, seven tunnels and an aqueduct beneath the Cromford Canal, while most of the line was carried on embankments or passed through cuttings.

The 1784-yard Clay Cross Tunnel marked the highest point of the whole line. Fifteen men died building it, possibly because of carelessness with blasting powder.

The tunnel saw one of the first uses of the absolute block signalling system. On double-tracked lines, which enabled trains to travel in one direction on each track, trains had to be spaced far enough apart so that they could not collide.

Today, the Derby to Chesterfield section of the North Midland is part of the Midland Main Line from St Pancras to Sheffield.

George Stephenson was appointed as engineer of the standard gauge York & North Midland Railway, and Royal Assent for the line was obtained on June 21, 1836. Robert Stephenson & Co supplied locomotives. The first 14½ miles from York to the Leeds & Selby Railway opened on May 29, 1839.

The final section of the York & North Midland, the length leading to the junction at Altofts with the North

East Midlands Trains Class 222 DMU No. 222005 leaving Clay Cross Tunnel in May 2010. PHIL SANGWELL*

Midland, opened at the end of June the following year; it was possible to leave York at 7.30am and be in London 14 hours later.

On July 31, 1854, the York & North Midland amalgamated with the Leeds Northern Railway and York, Newcastle & Berwick Railway, and formed the North Eastern Railway.

George Stephenson was also superintendent of the Manchester & Leeds Railway, which connected the two cities via the North Midland Railway. Its engineer was Thomas Longridge Gooch, a brother of Isambard Brunel's GWR locomotive superintendent Daniel Gooch.

The London & Blackwall Railway was operated by these massive cable winding drums, as pictured at Minories station in 1840. ILLUSTRATED LONDON NEWS

Robert Stephenson & Co supplied two 2-2-2s, named *Stephenson* and *La Fleche*, for continental Europe's first steam railway, the line between Brussels and Mechelen. Also, an example of the firm's Patentee 2-2-2 – an enlarged version of the *Planet* type which ran on the Liverpool & Manchester Railway – was built under licence by Cockerill at its Seraing works for use on the same line. Another patentee was shipped as a kit of parts to the Bavarian Ludwig Railway. It was named *Der Alder*, and although it was not the first steam locomotive to run in Germany, in 1835 it became the first to run in the country on a commercial basis. Scrapped in 1858, a working replica of *Der Alder* was built by the Deutsche Reichsbahn in 1935, and when not running, is housed in the DB Museum in Nuremberg. ROBIN JONES

A line from Stepney (now Limehouse) linking it with the Eastern Counties Railway at Bow was opened in 1849, known as the London and Blackwall Extension Railway (LBER), at which time the line was converted to steam locomotive operation and the track converted to 4ft 8½in gauge.

It was operational from 1840 until 1926 for passengers – later becoming part of the London Tilbury & Southend route to Fenchurch Street – and 1968 for freight, closing after the decline of inner London's docks. Much of its infrastructure was reused as part of the Docklands Light Railway.

FAME AND FORTUNE ABROAD

In 1835, leading Italian banker and iron producer Emanuele Fenzi financed the planned building of a 61-mile line between Florence, Pisa and the port of Livorno, Three years later, Robert was asked to direct the works.

The railway was one of the first in Italy, and in June 1841 was named Leopolda in honour of the Grand Duke. In August 1841, Robert was made Knight of the Order of Leopold for his improvements to locomotives.

The locomotives, track and infrastructure were all built by Robert and his company, including the bridge over the River Arno, which lasted for nearly a century.

The first test trains ran between Pisa to Livorno on January 27, 1844. On June 10, 1848, the whole route was opened throughout, and it brought an economic revolution to the region it served.

Russian prince and entrepreneur Anatole Demidoff and Polish prince Giuseppe Poniatowski were so impressed they commissioned Robert to build another line in Tuscany through the Muraglione Pass to Forli. The line was never built, but paved the way for the construction of the Faentina Railway four decades later.

Between 1837-40, Robert advised his friend, the French engineer Paulin Talabot, on the building of the Chemins de fer du Gard from Beauvoir to Alès.

Robert also travelled to Spain to provide advice on the building of the railway from the Bay of Biscay to Madrid.

In late 1850, the Swiss Federal Council consulted Robert on the country's future railway network.

In 1833, Pasha Muhammad Ali, the Albanian-born Ottoman vice-roy of Egypt, investigated the possibility of building a railway between Suez and Cairo to cut the shipping times between Europe and India. He was on the verge of authorising the line to be built when the French pressured him in to ditching the scheme in favour of a canal.

French social reformer Barthélemy Prosper Enfantin persuaded both Robert and Talabot to join the Société d' Études du Canal de Suez in 1846. The pair looked at the feasibility of building a modern waterway linking the Mediterranean to the Indian Ocean, a scheme first considered by Napoleon Bonaparte.

In 1851, Pasha Muhammad Ali's successor Abbas I, founder of the Muhammad Ali dynasty of Egypt and Sudan, asked Robert to build Egypt's first standard gauge railway. Robert was duly appointed engineer-in-chief to the Egyptian Railway between Alexandria and Cairo.

The first section, between Alexandria, on the Mediterranean coast, and Kafr El-Zayyat, on the Rosetta branch of the Nile, was opened in 1854. It was the first railway in the Ottoman Empire as well as Africa and the Middle East. The section between Kafr El-Zayyat and Cairo was completed in 1856, and two years later the line was extended to Suez.

Robert's railway was the first modern transport link between both seas, as the Suez Canal was not finished until 1869.

Also in 1851, Robert became engineer-in-charge of Norway's Hovedbanen or Hoved-jembane, the country's first public railway, running from Christiania (now Oslo) to Eidsvold, and opening on September 1, 1854. In 1855 Robert was decorated Knight of the Legion of Honour by the Emperor of France.

Having served as vice-president of the Institution of Civil Engineers since 1847, he was elected president in 1856, and the following year received a Honorary Doctorate of Civil Law at Oxford along with Brunel and Dr Livingstone.

Like Brunel, Robert Stephenson also conjectured the replacement of steam locomotives with alternative traction in the form of atmospheric propulsion. He sent assistants to the Dalkey Atmospheric Railway in Ireland to observe the system in operation, but advised against its use as the failure of one pump would bring traffic to a stop.

The replica of *Der Alder* carries a worksplate celebrating the Newcastle firm which designed it. ROBIN JONES

A BRIDGE BUILDER TO RIVAL BRUNEL

Isambard Brunel is today remembered as much for his magnificent bridges as for his railways.

Robert Stephenson learned much from his father in the field of bridge construction, but took the art several stages further. The Chester & Holyhead Railway was designed to carry the Irish Mail from Holyhead to London.

Following the opening of the Liverpool & Manchester, Grand Junction and London & Birmingham railways, Holyhead had lost out on this trade. With a new journey time of 22½ hours from London to Dublin, from January 24, 1839, the Irish Mail contract was switched to Liverpool.

The Chester & Holyhead Railway board appointed George Stephenson to survey the route and draw up plans for the new line. His route was designed for speed; taking the railway west from Chester along the North Wales coast he was able to plan wide curves and long, straight sections of line that avoided the hills of Snowdonia and therefore any steep gradients.

The Chester & Holyhead Railway Act received Royal Assent on July 4, 1844. The company appointed Robert Stephenson as chief engineer to build the 85 miles of double track railway.

The board then submitted a Bill to Parliament for the line between Ogwen and Llanfair PG, including the bridging of no less than the Menai Strait. The

contract was eventually won by Thomas Brassey, in partnership with William McKenzie Ross and Robert Stephenson.

The first sod was cut and the initial blasting shot fired at Conwy Tunnel on St David's Day, March 1, 1845, the same year work started on the coastal tunnels at Llandegai, Belmont, Bangor ,and Penmaenbach.

The building of the line presented many formidable challenges, not least of all coastal erosion – echoes of Brunel's South Devon Railway here.

The tunnel was opened in November 1846 amid local celebration. In October 1846, the sea defences had been breached at Penmaenmawr Tunnel entrances and the trackbed washed away while still under construction.

The rebuilt Britannia Bridge crossing the Menai Straits, reconstructed after the original was destroyed by a fire in 1970. ROBIN JONES

LMS Royal Scot 4-6-0 No. 46138 *The London Irish Rifleman* exits the southern side of Robert Stephenson's Britannia Bridge over the Menai Straits in July 1962. POLYRUS*

The pair of monumental lions guarding the southern entrance to Britannia Bridge, as seen in a contemporary sketch. A pair were also sited at the northern approach. They survive today, beneath the deck of the A55 road, which crosses the rebuilt bridge, but cannot be seen from the roadway.

THE WORLD'S FIRST TUBULAR BRIDGE

Much of Robert Stephenson's time, however, was devoted to the design of the vital major bridges on the route, beginning with the crossing of the River Conwy at Conwy.

Scottish civil engineer, structural engineer and shipbuilder William Fairburn, who had been retained by Robert Stephenson as a consultant on the Chester & Holyhead Railway, came up with the idea of a rectangular tube or box girder to bridge the wide river estuary.

Engineers Easton & Amos built a set of hydraulic engines to lift the 1300-ton bridge girder into place, an operation which began on March 6, 1848.

Completed that year and officially opened in 1849, it was the world's first tubular bridge, running parallel to Thomas Telford's Gothic suspension bridge, which had opened in 1826.

Its innovative design, featuring wrought-iron box-section tubes, provided the ultimate in strength and flexibility.

Magnificent as it was, the Conwy Bridge was really a dry run for a far bigger project, the Britannia Bridge, spanning the Menai Straits, essential if Holyhead was to be reached by rail uninterrupted.

Robert Stephenson built the Britannia Bridge with two main 460ft spans comprising rectangular iron tubes supported by masonry piers, the centre one built on the Britannia Rock. The box sections were assembled on shore before being floated into position and lifted into place. Two additional 230ft spans made up the bridge, a 1511ft-long continuous girder, with the railway running inside the tubes.

Before then, the longest wrought iron span had been 31ft, and so the Britannia Bridge was hailed as a technological marvel, having pushed forward the boundaries of railway engineering – just as Isambard Brunel did at Maidenhead and elsewhere.

Before the railway arrived, the town of Menai Bridge was known as

The three bridges at Conway, as seen from Conwy Castle, from left to right: Road, pedestrian and rail, the latter designed by Robert Stephenson. JAMES PETTS

Porthaethwy and was one of the main ferry crossing points. It now expanded to house construction workers.

It took four years to build the bridge, which opened on March 5, 1850. The tubular bridge as a concept, while widely praised in engineering circles, proved too expensive for widespread use owing to the cost of the colossal amount of wrought iron needed.

Fairbairn went on to develop wrought iron trough bridges which used some of the ideas he had developed in the tubular bridges on the Chester & Holyhead Railway.

The Britannia Bridge was severely damaged by fire on May 23, 1970, when two boys who claimed they had been looking for birds inside the box girder dropped a burning torch inside it.

The bridge was totally rebuilt and now has two levels, trains running below and the A55 road on top.

Since the rebuilding, Conwy railway bridge remains the only surviving example of Robert Stephenson's tubular bridge construction.

LEFT: Robert Stephenson's box-section Britannia Bridge as seen in a contemporary sketch from 1852.

RIGHT: A wrought iron section of Robert Stephenson's original Britannia Bridge, preserved alongside the rebuilt version.

A CANADIAN FIRST

Robert Stephenson adapted the design for the 1.9-mile Victoria Bridge over the St Lawrence River at Montreal.

The Victoria Bridge connects Montreal to the city of Saint-Lambert on the south shore. It was the first to span the St Lawrence River. The railway runs through the middle with roadways on either side, and has 24 ice-breaking supports. The big problem with crossing the river before the bridge was built was the fact it freezes over in winter.

While it was possible to cross by boat in summer and sled in winters, conditions at other times of the year, particularly with meltwaters in the spring, made it particularly treacherous.

The original deck was a long tubular bridge, designed by Robert Stephenson and British bridge builder Alexander McKenzie Ross, engineer for the Grand Trunk Railway which ran over it, and assembled from pre-fabricated sections made in England. The contractors were the British partnership of Peto, Brassey and Betts. Completed in 1859, the first goods train ran over it on December 12 that year and the first passenger train five days later. In its day, it was the longest bridge in the world.

The bridge was officially opened by Albert, Prince of Wales, the future Edward VII, on August 25, 1860.

In 1897/1898, the metal tube from 1860 was replaced by metal trusses, and the tube was demolished. The stone piers from the original remain in use.

BELOW: Canada's Victoria Bridge seen from Île-des-Sœurs, with Jacques-Cartier Bridge in the background. When completed, Robert Stephenson's structure was the longest in the world, beating any bridge distance achieved by Isambard Brunel. EMDX*

DISASTER AT DEE BRIDGE

One spectacular failure on the Chester & Holyhead Railway and a black mark on his career was Robert Stephenson's Dee Bridge, near Chester.

It had been completed in September 1846, and opened for local traffic after approval by the first Railway Inspector, General Charles Pasley. Stephenson had designed it using cast-iron girders, each of which was made of three large castings dovetailed together. Each girder was strengthened by wrought-iron bars.

However, one of its three 98ft cast iron spans collapsed on May 24, 1847 as a local train from Ruabon ran over it at about 30mph and fell through, leaving three passengers, two mail coach drivers, the train guard, and the fireman dead, and nine other people seriously injured. The Illustrated London News reported: "The sudden shock and concussion rendered almost all the persons in the carriages totally insensible of their situation. One man, indeed, named Proud, recovered himself almost immediately; he found himself in a carriage turned upside down in the river, and, being fully sensible of the horrors of his situation, he exerted himself to the utmost, and succeeded in getting through the carriage window, whence he precipitated himself into the river, and swam ashore.

"The train consisted of one first-class carriage, two second class carriages, and a luggage-van; but it is stated that there were not more than two dozen passengers. The train was proceeding as usual along the line, had already crossed two of the arches, and was in the act of crossing the third, when, without one moment's warning, all the carriages were precipitated into the river, a depth of about 30 feet; the engine and tender, which had crossed the bridge, pursuing their course along the line.

"The crash was heard at a great distance, and assistance was promptly on the spot, Mr. Jones, the house surgeon of the Infirmary, being very active in rendering every aid to the unfortunate sufferers. In a brief space of time four dead bodies were taken out of the river, and 12 or 13 of the passengers, who were more or less wounded, were extricated from their perilous situation, and conveyed to the Infirmary."

The guard, George Roberts, "met an instantaneous death, having been precipitated from the top of the carriage on to the bank of the river, amid the falling ruins".

The engine driver, a Mr Clayton, said that when passing over the third span from Chester, he felt the rails sinking beneath him, and he instantly put on the steam, and then felt the carriages severed, while the engine and tender cleared the bridge, and reached the abutments on the Wrexham or south bank of the river in safety, but the jerk or wrench arising from this severance threw the tender off the rails, inclining it sideways towards the stone parapet.

The tender was finally thrown somewhat on its side, and about three feet off the rails, on the east side; this shock severing it from the engine, the iron bar or hook connecting them being snapped in two. "The stoker, whose name is Anderson, was by this shock thrown off the tender upon the rails, and

The aftermath of the Dee Bridge disaster – the design of the structure was condemned by a Royal Commission.

the screw-jack from the tender falling on him, killed him on the spot," said the report. At the ensuing inquest, Robert Stephenson was accused of negligence, because cast iron was known to be brittle in tension or bending.

The investigation that followed was one of the first major inquiries conducted by the newly formed Railway Inspectorate. A report compiled by lead investigator Captain John Lintorn Arabin Simmons, of the Royal Engineers, suggested that repeated flexing of the girder had weakened the bridge significantly.

He discovered the main girder had broken in two places, the first break occurring at the centre, while driving a locomotive across the remaining girders proved they moved by several inches under the load.

Simmons claimed Stephenson's design was basically flawed, and the wrought iron trusses fixed to the girders did not do anything to reinforce the girders. The inquest jury agreed with him.

Stephenson argued the locomotive derailed while crossing the bridge, and the impact force against the girder caused it to break, but witnesses claimed the girder fractured first.

An extra load of ballast that had just been laid over the track as a fire-prevention measure may also have contributed to the fracture.

Following the inquest, a Royal Commission condemned the design and the use of trussed cast iron, which had been used to great effect in the Crystal Palace in London, as well as in railway bridges. The Dee Bridge was later rebuilt using wrought iron.

The Chester & Holyhead Railway began running passenger trains over the 60 miles from Chester to Bangor May 1, 1848, and across the Britannia Bridge to Holyhead on March 18, 1850.

Looking down river in Newcastle-upon-Tyne: In the foreground is the High Level Bridge. MATTHEW SMITH

HITTING NEW HEIGHTS IN NEWCASTLE

Not only did Robert Stephenson link the island of Anglesey to the mainland by rail, but built two structures which allowed through rail journeys from England to Scotland.

For the York, Newcastle & Berwick Railway, he designed the High Level Bridge over the River Tyne at Newcastle as a two-deck bridge supported on tall stone columns, with rail traffic carried on the upper deck and road traffic on the lower deck.

It was an improved version of Britannia Bridge. Despite the fact High Level Bridge was designed afterwards, it was completed before it.

Built between 1847-49, at a total cost of £491,153, it is the first major example of a wrought iron-tied arch or bowstring girder bridge.

Spanning 1337ft, it stands up to 131ft above the river. There are six spans over the river and four on land.

Single carriageway road and pedestrian walkways occupy the lower deck of the spans, and the railway the upper deck.

A cornerstone in the connection of the English and Scottish railway systems, its completion enabled trains to run from London to Edinburgh for the first time.

Rail traffic began using it on August 15, 1849, but it was officially opened on September 27 that year by Queen Victoria, and brought into regular use on February 4, 1850.

It was not the first scheme to build a high-level bridge over the Tyne at this point. Newcastle master mason Edward Hutchinson produced a scheme to build one in 1771 after the old Tyne Bridge was washed away, but it came to nothing. B R Dodd, a local civil engineer, drew up a blueprint for an elevated suspension bridge in 1833, and six years later, John and Benjamin Green produced their plan, which despite mustering support also came to nothing.

Newcastle builder Richard Grainger, who in the early 19th century before the coming of the railway was a key figure in the redevelopment of Newcastle town centre, wanted to build a superstructure on the Tyne Bridge, supported on metal tubes resting on the piers.

The big flaw in this scheme was that it would have left the railway disconnected.

Architect John Dobson, who worked with Grainger on the town centre redevelopment, came up with a better scheme.

His bridge plan included a double-track railway as well as a road.

Robert Stephenson's design of the High Level Bridge influenced none other than Isambard Brunel when he drew up plans for the Royal Albert Bridge, which spanned the River Tamar at Saltash and opened in 1859.

In 1906, the King Edward VII Bridge – 500 yards upstream – was completed, solving the main problem of the High Level Bridge in that trains entering Newcastle Centre station from the south had to be reversed back across the bridge when returning in that direction.

Also, engines had to switch ends before a train could head north towards Edinburgh.

The new bridge became part of the East Coast Main Line, with the High Level Bridge, downgraded to handling local services to Sunderland, Middlesbrough and the now-closed Leamside Line.

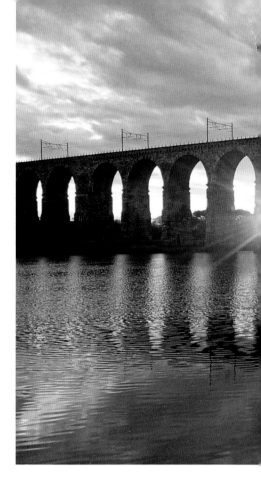

SPANNING THE BORDER

Robert Stephenson's second major structure linking London to Edinburgh was the 28-arch Royal Border Bridge over the River Tweed, built for the York, Newcastle & Berwick Railway.

When Queen Victoria opened it in 1850, passengers could travel from London to Edinburgh by the same railway line for the first time.

On July 4, 1838, the Edinburgh & Glasgow Railway received statutory powers to build Scotland's first inter-city line. The first passenger services between Edinburgh Haymarket and Glasgow Queen Street ran on February 21, 1842.

Six weeks before the Edinburgh & Glasgow opened, its chairman, John Learmonth, held a meeting with a group of Edinburgh gentlemen, who were keen on building a railway running eastwards to the fishing port of Dunbar, 30 miles away. They decided to promote such a scheme as the North British Railway.

Local investors were unconvinced that a line running only to Dunbar would pay, and wanted it to run further – across the border into England.

It was decided to build a line all the way to Berwick-on-Tweed. Now backed by many English investors, the North British Railway was approved by Parliament on July 4, 1844 with little opposition.

The building of Berwick station in 1847 involved the demolition of the great hall of 12th-century Berwick Castle, where Edward I took oaths of allegiance from Scottish nobility in 1296.

Huge celebrations marked the North British Railway's first operations on

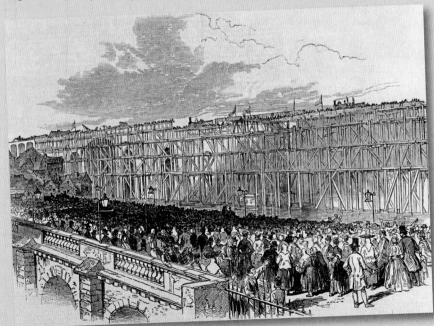

The opening of High Level Bridge at Newcastle-upon-Tyne.

The Royal Border Bridge spans the River Tweed between Berwick-upon-Tweed and Tweedmouth in Northumberland. It is a Grade I-listed railway viaduct built between 1847 and 1850, when it was opened by Queen Victoria. TOM PARNELL*

June 18, 1846, when two new 0-4-2s hauled two maroon-liveried trains out of Edinburgh.

Regular services began four days later, with five trains each way between Edinburgh and Berwick, from where there were stagecoach connections to Newcastle. However, the North British Railway killed off stagecoach services over its route at a stroke.

Meanwhile, the Newcastle & Berwick Railway arrived at the south bank of the River Tweed in March 1847, linking Berwick to the Brandling Junction Railway at Gateshead.

At first, a temporary viaduct was built across the river to allow through running.

It was superseded in July 1850 when Queen Victoria opened Robert Stephenson's Royal Border Bridge.

The 28-arch brick-built and stone-faced structure is 2162ft long and stands 126ft above the river, three miles south of the actual border.

In 1847, the Newcastle & Berwick Railway merged with the York & Newcastle Railway to become the York, Newcastle and Berwick Railway.

One of the most impressive structures on the entire East Coast Main Line, the Grade 1-listed bridge underwent significant repairs in the 1990s with the help of funding from English Heritage. In 2010, the bridge was fitted with colour-changing lights to mark its 160th anniversary.

OTHER BRIDGES

Robert Stephenson also built a swing bridge across the navigable River Nene at Sutton Bridge in Lincolnshire.

It replaced an earlier timber and cast

A lock of Robert Stephenson's hair is held in the National Railway Museum's collection at York. ROBIN JONES

iron bridge built in 1831 by John Rennie the Younger and Thomas Telford. It opened in the middle, like London's Tower Bridge.

However, it was decided its siting was awkward and Stephenson was called in to design a replacement, which opened in 1850.

Stephenson's bridge was used only for road traffic until 1864 when the Midland Railway obtained powers to also use it for rail traffic. It was superseded in 1897 by the present-day Crosskeys Bridge, built to serve both road and rail.

While it had been intended to leave Stephenson's bridge in position, the river navigation authorities objected to having the obstacle of two swing bridges in close proximity, so it was removed.

For the Ulverston & Lancaster Railway, Robert Stephenson built the 552-yard Arnside Viaduct to span the River Kent in Cumbria in 1857. Rebuilt in 1915, the 50-pier viaduct is today part of the Cumbrian coast route.

Carlo Marochetti's statue of Robert Stephenson stands outside Euston station. ROBIN JONES

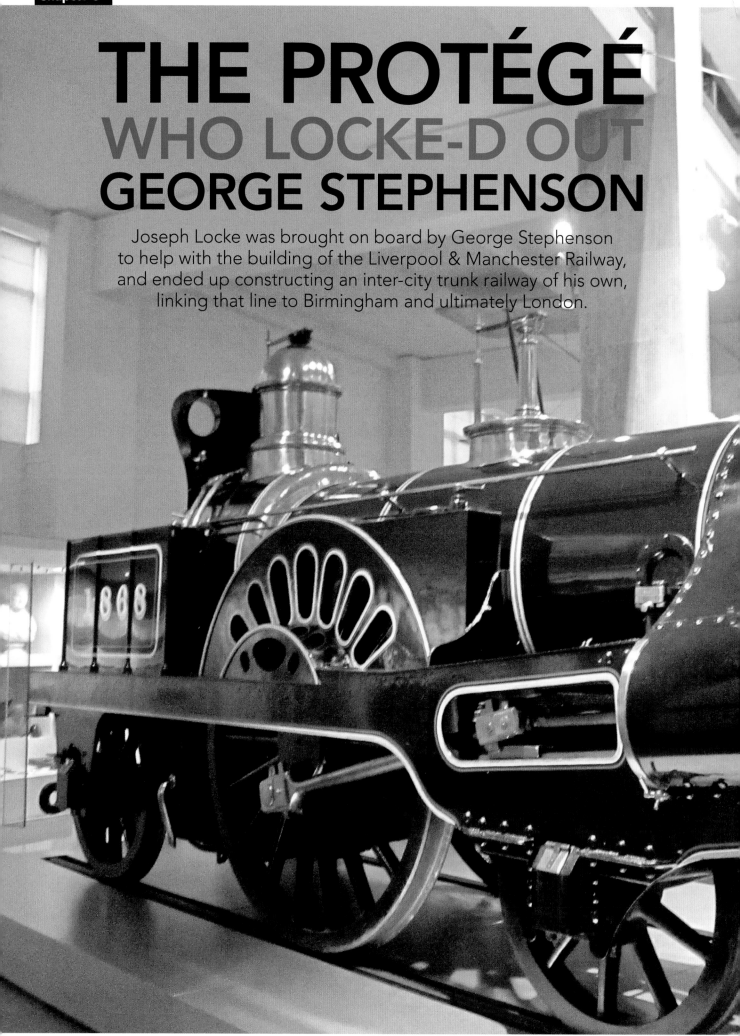

Chapter 8

THE PROTÉGÉ
WHO LOCKE-D OUT
GEORGE STEPHENSON

Joseph Locke was brought on board by George Stephenson to help with the building of the Liverpool & Manchester Railway, and ended up constructing an inter-city trunk railway of his own, linking that line to Birmingham and ultimately London.

Grand Junction Railway 2-2-2 No. 49 *Columbine* on display in the Science Museum. Designed by Alexander Allen, it was built at Crewe Works in 1845, and withdrawn in 1902. ROBIN JONES

Railway builder Joseph Locke was responsible for three-quarters of today's West Coast Main Line.

O n August 9, 1805, Joseph Locke was born in Attercliffe, near Sheffield. By 1823, at the age of 17, having served an apprenticeship in Tyneside – partially under his father William, a manager at Walbottle Colliery – he had become an accomplished mining engineer, who could carry out surveys, sink shafts, maintain stationary engines, bore tunnels... and construct railways.

That year, George Stephenson was drawing up plans for the Stockton & Darlington Railway. He and his son Robert visited William Locke and his son at Barnsley and arranged for Joseph to work for them at their new Forth Street locomotive works in Newcastle.

Joseph impressed very quickly, and established a position of authority. He and Robert Stephenson became close friends.

After George Stephenson undertook the original survey of the Liverpool & Manchester Railway, his findings were found to be flawed, and so another survey was undertaken by engineer Charles Vignoles.

The directors asked Joseph Locke to repeat the survey of the proposed tunnel works, but a report was highly critical of the work that had been carried out and placed George Stephenson in a bad light. Somewhat surprisingly, Stephenson continued to employ Locke, probably because he was too good to let go, and when Stephenson was appointed engineer of the L&MR, he appointed Joseph Locke as his assistant to work alongside Vignoles.

Locke fell out with Vignoles, who resigned, and then took over responsibility for the western half of the line. Some historians believe it was Locke rather than George Stephenson who came up with the solution to the Chat Moss peat bog obstacle.

It was Locke who collaborated with Robert Stephenson on a report to the L&MR directors, which argued locomotives rather than stationary engines were the right way ahead, and this led to the decision to hold the Rainhill Trials.

The coat of arms of the Grand Junction Railway.

With the Horse Bridge over the River Weaver in the foreground, LMS 'Black Five' 4-6-0s No. 44871 and 45407 are seen crossing Dutton Viaduct bound for Bristol on November 17, 2016. ANDREW*

NEXT STOP BIRMINGHAM!

In 1823, businessmen in Birmingham and Liverpool formed a committee to build a railway between the two cities under the banner of the Birmingham & Liverpool Railroad Company.

Basic surveys were undertaken in 1825 under the direction of George Stephenson who, even by then, convinced that the future of transport lay with steam locomotives, had started drawing up plans for a national rail network.

In a prospectus, George and Robert

The five-arch Grade II-listed Vale Royal Viaduct crossing the River Weaver was started before George Stephenson left the Grand Junction Railway, and took 700 men two-and-a-half years to build.

Stephenson were named as engineers, with George's brother Robert as secretary.

However, the scheme failed, because the promoters fought shy of conflict with the powerful canal owners whose trade would be sorely threatened; it has been said Birmingham has more miles of inland waterway than Venice. Furthermore, at the time there was a trade depression, and steam railways had yet to be proven as a sound financial investment.

The imminent completion of the L&MR opened up an entirely

new scenario. In 1829, as George Stephenson's assistant, Locke was given the task of surveying a route for the proposed Grand Junction Railway, which would bring Britain's second city, Birmingham, into the L&MR remit.

Not only that, it would link to the proposed London & Birmingham Railway, giving Liverpool's port direct rail access to the capital.

However, Liverpool businessmen wanted a more direct route, and Vignoles re-emerged to survey a route which included a Mersey tunnel and

a line to Chester, where it would join George Stephenson's proposed route of 1825.

Yet the idea of a tunnel under a major river was still unproven, and Vignoles was jumping too far ahead of his time for the Liverpool investors. Work had begun four years earlier on Marc Brunel's ground-breaking Thames Tunnel, but that would not be completed until 1843.

One day there would be tunnels below the Mersey, but for now it was Locke's route that was chosen. The proposed railway was to run from Dallam, in Warrington, making an end-on junction with the short Warrington & Newton Railway, a branch of the L&M via Warrington, a tiny rural village called Crewe, Stafford and Wolverhampton to Birmingham. It was Locke who is said to have chosen Crewe as the site for the line's locomotive, carriage and wagon works.

On May 6, 1833, enabling Acts for both the Grand Junction and the London & Birmingham Railway were passed by Parliament. George Stephenson, who had friends on the board, assumed the job of chief engineer would be his. However, Locke's contract with Stephenson at the L&MR had run out, and he decided he would apply for the job, too.

During the building of the L&MR, George Stephenson had demonstrated a lack of ability in organising major civil engineering projects. By contrast, Locke's ability to manage complex projects was well known. He offered detailed planning, efficient management and a method that would run like clockwork, whereas George Stephenson operated by making spontaneous decisions, failing to consult others and without keeping proper records.

Stephenson's undeniable ace up his sleeve, however, was his track record of success, a seemingly perfect answer to his critics.

Locke had been hoping for the top job, and threatened to walk away from the Grand Junction, but the directors, who desperately wanted to retain his services, while not upsetting George Stephenson, arrived at a compromise solution whereby Locke was made responsible for the northern half of the line with Stephenson being in charge of the southern half.

Initial work began on the Grand Junction with the building of the 10-mile Weaver Valley section, to the west of Northwich, where Locke had to build two crossings over the river.

Elsewhere, by 1834, it had become clear there were problems with the southern section of the route, largely caused by delays in letting contracts for its construction. It seemed George Stephenson had repeated his mistakes made when beginning work on the

Built on the site of a rural farming community, Crewe station opened in 1843 and became one of the most famous railway works and junctions in the world.

L&MR, by delegating work to far less able subordinates who let him down. This time around there was far greater criticism.

The company directors wrote to George Stephenson after he failed to attend board meetings, submit reports, reply to letters or produce recommendations as regards to the trackwork. Contractors had no clear set of specifications on which to bid, whereas Locke had the contracts let for every stage of his northern section by September 25, 1834.

Locke was then asked to step in on the southern section, and rapidly came up with a satisfactory report.

The railway company lost patience with Stephenson, but tried to compromise by making both men joint engineers. Stephenson's pride would not let him accept this, and so he resigned from the project, and by autumn of 1835 Locke had become chief engineer for the whole of the line. A rift developed and severely strained his friendship with Robert, and in the wake of the conflict, Locke suffered a breakdown through nervous exhaustion, and was absent from the building of the line for

several months. However, he remained determined to have the Grand Junction open by the summer of 1837.

Locke had always been under George Stephenson's shadow, but from this point, he stood alone, and would be his own man, and stand or fall by his own achievements.

In sole charge, Locke divided the project into a few large sections rather than many small ones. This approach allowed him to work closely with his contractors to develop the best methods, overcome problems and personally gain practical experience of the building process and of the contractors themselves. He decided to avoid major civil engineering works where possible, although they could not be avoided altogether. The principal one was the superb 60ft-high and 500-yard long 20-arch Dutton Viaduct, which crosses the River Weaver and the Weaver Navigation in Cheshire.

Other viaducts were built at Warrington and Vale Royal, with an aqueduct at Preston Brook carrying the Bridgewater Canal over the railway.

Locke reviewed several of the contracts on the southern section

The Grand Junction Railway was said to have built the first 2-4-0s. This example, *Atlas*, was outshopped from Crewe in 1845.

following Stephenson's departure.

In the case of Penkridge Viaduct, across the River Penk between Wolverhampton and Stafford, he found the lowest tender of £26,000, which had been submitted under the Stephenson reign, was grossly inflated, and the job could be adequately done for £6000.

Engineer Thomas Brassey, then 29, was the same age as Locke, who persuaded him to enter the field of railway construction. He was appointed as builder of Penkridge Viaduct and its approach embankments, and became his first railway structure. Brassey went on to become one of the world's greatest railway engineers of the 19th century.

With trackwork, George and Robert Stephenson used horse tramway-fashion single-stone blocks on which to mount the rails, as seen on the Stockton & Darlington.

Locke, however, preferred wooden sleepers, as they offered a smoother ride.

The Grand Junction was first laid as a temporary measure with sleepers, but much of them were subsequently replaced by stone blocks. In 1845, 62 miles were laid on stone blocks and 20 miles on sleepers, but gradually Locke's system won the day, rendering the Stephensons' blocks obsolete.

Thomas Brassey's Penkridge Viaduct has seven arches and foundations that were buried in concrete to a depth of 70ft. The first train crossed Penkridge Viaduct on June 1, 1837 as a test, and on July 4, 1837 it was officially opened. MICK MALPASS*

Thomas Brassey (October 7, 1805-December 8, 1870) was an English civil engineering contractor and manufacturer of building materials, who was responsible for building most of the world's railways in the 19th century. He was given his big break by Joseph Locke, who hired him to build the Grand Junction Railway's Penkridge Viaduct. He went on to far bigger projects, and by 1847, Brassey had built about one-third of the railways in Britain; by the time of his death, in 1870, he had built one in 20 miles of railway in the world. He was active in the development of steamships (like Isambard Brunel), mines, locomotive factories, marine telegraphy, and water supply and sewage systems. He built part of the London sewerage system.

LOCKE'S BIG DAY

The Grand Junction was the first trunk railway to be completed in England. It also claimed to be the world's first long-distance railway with steam traction.

On June 1, 1837, a group of the railway's directors made a private trip along the route from Liverpool to Wolverhampton, taking 3½ hours. The entire board made its own trip on June 24, all the way to Vauxhall, the temporary Birmingham terminus that held the fort before the 28-arch viaduct over the valley of the River Rea was built to link it to the London & Birmingham Railway's Curzon Street station.

The rail was formally opened on July 4, 1837, with trains running from both ends of the line and crowds thronging the route.

The decorations on the inaugural trains were toned down because William IV had died on June 20, and his funeral did not take place until July 8, so the country was in mourning. Therefore the railway was opened without the pomp and ceremony that had been seen on the first days of the Stockton & Darlington and Liverpool and Manchester.

The first train out of Vauxhall departed at 7am, headed by Robert Stephenson & Company's 2-2-2 No. 8 *Wild Fire*, and comprising eight named carriages: *Triumph, Greyhound, Swallow, Liverpool & Birmingham Mail, Celerity, Umpire, Statesman and Birmingham & Manchester Mail*.

Out of the suburbs and into countryside (that is today inner-city Birmingham), the train reached 30mph on the Aston embankment and 40mph at Newton Road station.

At Warrington the train was divided, with one half being taken on to Manchester by a waiting engine. Both Liverpool and Manchester were reached at 11.30am. The 97-mile journey had

taken 4½ hours at an average speed of 22mph. A second-class train departed Vauxhall at 8.30am for Liverpool.

At 11.30pm, a train comprising carriages from trains that had left Liverpool and Manchester at 6.30pm arrived half an hour late at Vauxhall, the delay caused by crowds at the stops en route.

In the 19th century, industrial Birmingham was hailed as the workshop of the world. Locke's railway had just brought that world so much nearer. He had joined the elite group of railway engineers who had connected one city to another, and in doing so formed the basis of today's national rail network.

At 7pm, the first return train from Liverpool reached Vauxhall. A mixed first and second-class train, which should have reached Vauxhall by 10pm, did not arrive until 3am the following day, because of a boiler tube breaking.

While the L&MR had reached agreement to carry mail in 1830, the Grand Junction became the first railway to carry mail under contract for the Post Office. The introduction of mail coaches in the era of the 'penny post' was another major nail in the coffin of the road coach operators.

In 1840 the Grand Junction absorbed the Chester and Crewe Railway, before the latter operation. Now considering itself as part of a semi-national railway network, the company encouraged the development of the North Union Railway, which extended the tracks onward to Preston, and it also invested in the Lancaster & Carlisle Railway and the Caledonian Railway.

In 1845, the Grand Junction merged with the Liverpool and Manchester Railway, and consolidated its position by buying the North Union in association with the Manchester & Leeds Railway. It later became part of the London & North Western Railway, and in turn the LMS.

HORIZONS FURTHER AFIELD

While both George and Robert Stephenson were prepared to go to great lengths to avoid steep gradients that would burden the locomotives of the day – and as outlined in Chapter 6, Isambard Brunel sought to build a line using atmospheric traction to avoid his steam fleet having to tackle the South Devon banks – Locke showed more confidence in the ability of modern locomotives.

For the Lancaster & Carlisle Railway, George Stephenson proposed a circuitous route that avoided the Lake District altogether by taking a much longer route around Morecambe Bay and west Cumberland, saying climbing Shap Fell was out of the question.

By contrast, Locke was of the Brunel mould, pushing technology to the theoretical boundaries. His plan for the Lancaster & Carlisle used steep gradients and passed over Shap Fell – and was the one adopted by the line's director.

Locke argued that by avoiding long routes and tunnelling, the line could be finished more quickly, with less capital costs, and could start earning revenue sooner.

He took the same approach when drawing up plans for the Caledonian Railway from Carlisle to Glasgow (and later Edinburgh), which also had 1-in-75 gradients. In so many ways, he was fast

One of the Caledonian Railway's most glamorous locomotives, 1906-built 903 class 4-6-0 No. 903 *Cardean*, heads a Glasgow-bound dining car express over Beattock Summit, as depicted in a hand-coloured postcard.

proving he was the next generation from George Stephenson, the Father of the Railways.

Distinctive features of his works were economy, the use of masonry bridges wherever possible, and the absence of tunnels: there is none on his lines between Birmingham and Glasgow. However, Shap Fell remains the legendary severe test of any steam locomotive on the West Coast Main Line.

Locke was engaged to build the Manchester & Sheffield Railway, replacing Vignoles as chief engineer, after the latter had suffered financial difficulties.

Building the line led to the deaths of 32 of the 1000 or so navvies who toiled on it, and after delays it opened on December 23, 1845.

The line included Locke's 'Box Tunnel equivalent' in the shape of the three-mile Woodhead Tunnel, which not only George Stephenson claimed was an impossible feat, but said he would eat the first locomotive that got through the tunnel. It was estimated the mortality rate among the navvies at Woodhead Tunnel was just over 3%, whereas the mortality among soldiers at the Battle of Waterloo was just 2.11%.

Locke also designed the Lancaster & Preston Junction Railway and the Glasgow, Paisley & Greenock Railway. He also worked on the London & Southampton Railway, which became the London & South Western Railway, designing the Nine Elms to Waterloo Viaduct, Richmond Bridge and Barnes Bridge across the River Thames, the 12-arch Quay Street Viaduct and the 16-arch Cams Hill Viaduct, both in Fareham, and tunnels at Micheldever.

He also planned and built numerous railways on the Continent, including the Paris to Le Havre link, the Dutch Rhenish Railway, and the Barcelona to Mataró line.

Locke also helped set up the first locomotive works in France.

However, his greatest legacy is

When opened in 1845, the first Woodhead Tunnel (left) was one of the world's longest tunnels and the first on the trans-Pennine route. A second tunnel, next to it, was completed in 1853. The third and larger one was built in the 1950s when the line was electrified. The route was closed in the 1970s.
ROBIN JONES

The coat of arms of the Caledonian Railway, which Locke also helped engineer.

Britain's West Coast Main Line, formed by the joining of the Caledonian, Lancaster & Carlisle, and Grand Junction railways to Robert Stephenson's London & Birmingham Railway. Around 75% of the route was planned and engineered by Locke.

Following the death of George Stephenson in August 1848, the friendship of Locke and Robert Stephenson was revived. When Robert Stephenson died in October 1859, Locke was a pallbearer at his funeral.

Locke was also on friendly terms with his other great engineering rival, Isambard Brunel, despite their great difference of opinion on gauges.

Locke served as President of the Institution of Civil Engineers between December 1857 and December 1859, and as MP for Honiton in 1847.

Locke died on September 18, 1860, apparently from appendicitis, while on a shooting holiday. He is buried in London's Kensal Green Cemetery.

Barnsley's Locke Park was dedicated to his memory by his wife Phoebe in 1862. It features a statue of Locke plus a 'folly' named Locke Tower.

THE END GAME

Isambard Brunel's 7ft 0¼in broad gauge offered so many advantages over rival systems – but was found to be sadly lacking in one – standardisation. It was impossible to travel or convey freight across the country outside Great Western Railway territory without changing trains, placing a limitation on the development of a national railway system, and herein lay the traffic flaw of the engineering giant's dreams.

There was little doubt that the rail network developed by Isambard Brunel's and Daniel Gooch's classes of broad gauge locomotives were in many respects superior to much of what at the time had been in use elsewhere.

On March 10, 1845, the world had seen nothing like it when Gooch himself drove Firefly class 2-2-2 *Actaeon* the 388 miles from Paddington to Exeter and back, averaging 41.5mph, helped somewhat by the flat terrain of much of the Bristol & Exeter Railway.

When George Stephenson and Isambard Brunel built their first inter-city railways, clearly there would have been much speculation as to the time when national rail network would be formed, linking together these early lines. When choosing the broad gauge for the Great Western Railway, Isambard must have been mindful that there would be a lack of interchangeability of his trains when their tracks met those laid to the Stephenson 4ft 8½in gauge.

It happened sooner than he might have predicted. In 1844, the broad-gauge Bristol & Gloucester Railway had opened, but Gloucester was already served by the 4ft 8½in standard gauge lines of the Birmingham & Gloucester Railway. This discrepancy resulted in a break of gauge that forced all passengers and goods to change trains if travelling between the South West and the North. Here was the beginning of the 'Gauge War'.

In 1845 – just a decade after the GWR was given its Royal Assent in Parliament – in response to growing controversy over the issue, a commission was established by the Government to decide which direction to take when guiding

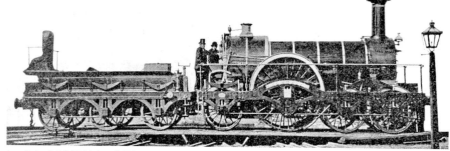

Iron Duke 4-2-2 *Lightning* of 1847, which registered 816,601 miles before withdrawal, a record for Gooch's class.

A panned shot of modern-day replica *Fire Fly* giving the impression of travelling at speed on the very short Didcot Railway Centre broad gauge track, just as the 62 original members of the class would have been capable of doing. FRANK DUMBLETON

were needed to pull a train, the same job could be done by a broad gauge one.

However, while the broad gauge had penetrated the west of England and South Wales, by and large the rest of the country was already dominated by the ever-expanding Stephenson gauge system. While 274 miles of broad gauge track had been laid, there were 1901 miles laid to 4ft 8½in.

It was also said that to widen 4ft 8½in gauge to broad gauge would be prohibitively expensive, especially at tunnels, while it would be a far less daunting task to narrow broad gauge.

Isambard challenged the findings and won some breathing space for his system. After the commission reported its findings, in August 1846, the Railway Regulation (Gauge) Act was passed which ordered by law all new railways in England, Scotland and Wales should be constructed to 4ft 8½in and in Ireland to 5ft 3in.

The Great Western Railway was allowed to continue with its 7ft 0¼in gauge in its current region, and not forced to narrow it, but was not to expand the system unless specific permission was first obtained. However, this was no victory for Brunel – it merely left the GWR system in isolation, with

future progress inhibited.

In 1846 the Bristol and Gloucester was bought by the Midland Railway and it was converted to standard gauge in 1854, which brought mixed-gauge track – whereby three rails allowed trains to run on either broad or standard gauge – into Bristol Temple Meads station.

The GWR extended into the West Midlands in competition with the Midland and the London & North Western Railway. Birmingham was reached via Oxford in 1852 and Wolverhampton in 1854, but its lines north of Oxford were built as mixed gauge.

Wolverhampton was the furthest north the broad gauge reached. That year the Shrewsbury and Birmingham Railway and the Shrewsbury and Chester Railway both amalgamated with the GWR, but these lines were standard gauge.

The GWR built its first Stephenson gauge engines in 1855, a year after absorbing its first 4ft 8½in lines. The mixed gauge was extended southwards from Oxford to Basingstoke at the end of 1856, and so allowed through goods traffic from the north of England to the South Coast via the London & South Western Railway.

the framework for a national network.

The Royal Commission on Railway Gauges was formed to choose between the broad gauge of the GWR and its allies, and the so-called 'narrow' of 4ft 8½in gauge used by most of the rest of the country. The Irish situation, where there were three gauges, was also considered.

Trials were held between two Stephenson gauge engines and Gooch's Firefly class *Ixion* - which recorded superior performances despite using less coke and water. Another 4ft 8½in-gauge competitor, the North Midland Railway's No. 54 *Stephenson*, ran off the line and toppled over after just 22 miles.

The commissioners heard that while broad gauge track was cheaper to build, it cost more to repair. Furthermore, Gooch demonstrated while his engines were more expensive to build, they were cheaper to repair. It was pointed out that whereby two 4ft 8½in-gauge locomotives

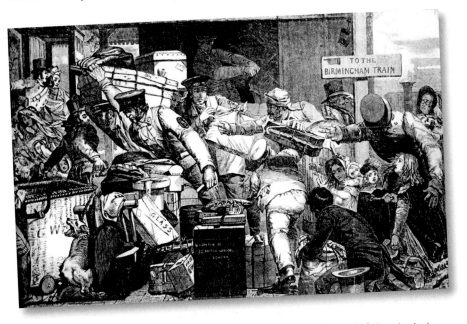

The hectic scenes at Gloucester where passengers had to change from a broad gauge train to a standard gauge one to make a through journey. ILLUSTRATED LONDON NEWS

The enormous tubular girder forming the eastern side of Isambard Brunel's bridge over the Tamar at Saltash is lifted into place.

BRUNEL'S LAST MASTERPIECE

On December 23, 1837, the standard gauge Hayle Railway in Cornwall, partially worked by steam, and in part by horses and rope-worked inclined planes, opened to take copper and tin ore from the Redruth and Camborne mining heartland to the ports of Hayle and Redruth. Passengers were carried on its main line between Hayle and Redruth from May 22, 1843.

This railway proved so successful that local businessmen looked at extending it at either end – to Penzance and Truro – and formed the West Cornwall Railway Company. At first it proposed using the 'atmospheric' system between Redruth and Truro.

A second and successful Bill received Royal Assent on August 3, 1846, giving the new company powers to buy the Hayle Railway, and to complete the route between Penzance and Truro.

The line was to be built to broad gauge, but at first, because of the collapse of 'Railway Mania', raising finance became difficult. When the

money did become available, it was decided to go for standard gauge, to save the expense of rebuilding the Hayle Railway. However, parliamentary powers obtained in 1850 were conditional on the West Cornwall laying 7ft 0¼in-gauge rails when given six months' notice from any connecting broad gauge line.

Isambard Brunel was appointed as engineer to the West Cornwall. Where viaducts were needed, they were built to Brunel's timber trestle design, which had been successful in crossing deep valleys in South Devon. By February 1852, the route between Redruth and Penzance was linked to the Hayle Railway.

A locomotive first appeared in Penzance station on February 25, and the line opened on March 11. The railway reached Higher Town on the western side of Truro on August 25, 1852.

After the railway was opened, passengers could travel from Penzance or Truro to Hayle, take the paddle steamer packet service to Bristol and travel eastwards via the GWR.

The important shipping port of

Falmouth did not want to be left out of the railway revolution, and in 1843, in advance of the South Devon Railway being completed, local businessmen W Tweedy and W H Bond asked the GWR to fund an extension into Cornwall.

The GWR told them to promote an independent scheme, and a prospectus for the Cornwall Railway appeared in 1844. It was to cross the Hamaoze, the tidal estuary of the Tamar at Torpoint, by ferry, and run via Liskeard, Lostwithiel, Par and St Austell to Truro and Falmouth.

The House of Lords rejected the scheme because of the Hamaoze ferry aspect, and Isambard was brought in as engineer to build a bridge across the Tamar. He chose a spot two miles north of Torpoint, and his broad gauge scheme received Royal Assent on August 3, 1846.

However, the 'Railway Mania' bubble had burst, and there was no money to build the line.

Brunel edited down the scheme, planning a single track for far less money. In January 1853, a £162,000 contract for construction of the bridge over the Tamar was let, yet because of the economic recession, a consortium of the GWR, Bristol & Exeter and South Devon railways agreed to lease the Cornwall line in return for guaranteeing bank loans.

Building of the railway again necessitated crossing numerous deep valleys, and all that could be afforded were Brunel's utilitarian timber trestle viaducts, which incurred heavy maintenance costs in the longer term. He built 34 timber viaducts over the 53 miles between Plymouth and Truro, each supported on masonry pillars.

However, try as he might to design one, there was no chance of a trestle bridge 'on the cheap' to cross the Tamar, a river estuary 1100ft and 70ft deep, especially as the navy demanded at least 100ft headroom to allow tall ships to safely pass below. Brunel then produced a radical blueprint involving a single-span bridge to clear the estuary in one go, but at a price. The estimated £500,000 cost was well out of the budget of the Cornwall Railway.

The final plans chosen were based around a pair of arched tubular girders, fastened to four cast-iron columns in the middle of the river, supported by the suspension of a pair of 450ft spans, which would carry a single-track railway from one side of the river to another. It was a development of his ground-breaking Usk bridge, at Chepstow, on the South Wales Railway.

The piers on the Cornwall side were completed in 1854, and the girders hauled up into position. The tubular girders were assembled on the east bank and weighed 1060 tons when finished. They were floated across the river into position on pontoons after a special dock was cut in the Devon bank. Crowds gathered to watch the spans raised into position. The 730-yard bridge took seven years to build – even longer than Box Tunnel – and cost £225,000,

Members of the Cornwall Railway made an inspection of their bridge by train on April 11, 1859. Nine days later, it underwent a statutory inspection, and tests by Colonel Yolland, on behalf of the Board of Trade, determined the bridge was "highly satisfactory".

East of the bridge, the Cornwall Railway bought the South Devon's branch from Millbay to Devonport, which had opened in 1849, and extended it to reach the new line.

On May 2, 1859, the bridge was formally opened by the Prince Consort, hence its title of the Royal Albert Bridge.

The mayors of Truro and Penzance arrived by train and were presented to the prince. A grand civic banquet was held in the Town Hall at Truro the next day, guests travelling on a special train from Plymouth. Two days later, the railway opened throughout to the public.

Sadly, Isambard was missing from all of these proceedings, because by now his health was failing fast. He did, however, see his magnificent bridge, taking a ride over it on a couch mounted on a truck a few days later, the train being pulled by a locomotive designed by Daniel Gooch.

THE DEATHS OF BRUNEL AND HIS RIVALS

Despite being diagnosed with a kidney problem, Isambard had been working hard on a steamship which would be twice the size of the ss *Great Britain*, one which would eventually be named

The monument to Isambard Kingdom Brunel on the Embankment in London. MATT BROWN*

the ss *Great Eastern*.

Not only did he miss the celebrations to mark the opening of the Royal Albert Bridge, but he was absent from a celebratory banquet held to mark the completion of the ship on August 5, 1859.

Isambard desperately wanted to go on the maiden voyage, and visited the ship on September 2 , but after two hours, he collapsed following a heart attack and had to be taken to his Duke Street home.

The maiden voyage began on September 7, but confined to bed, he had to settle for receiving news of his ship, which brought out crowds as it passed every coastal town between London and Holyhead.

May 20, 1892, saw the last broad gauge 'Cornishman' leave Paddington at 10.15am, bringing the curtain down on the first phase of Great Western Railway history as Isambard Kingdom Brunel's remarkable 7ft 0¼in-gauge system finally succumbed to standardisation.

He wrote to the GWR directors asking them to give all the workers at Swindon the day off along with special passes so they could ride to Weymouth by train and see his ship when it arrived. It was the final letter he wrote.

Isambard was horrified to hear about an explosion on board which killed five stokers as it passed Dungeness on September 8.

He called his family together for the last time, and died a few hours later, on September 15, 1859, aged just 53.

His funeral, attended by a large contingent of GWR staff, took place at Kensal Green Cemetery in London on September 20, when he was laid to rest in the same tomb as his mother and father.

The words I.K. BRUNEL, ENGINEER, 1859 appear in large metal letters on either end of the Royal Albert Bridge, added as a memorial after his death.

His death was followed soon afterwards by that of his arch rivals Robert Stephenson, on October 12, and Joseph Locke, on September 18, 1850. All three engineers died between 53 and 56 years of age, a circumstance attributed by transport historian Tom Rolt to their workaholic natures, each accomplishing more in their brief lives than most achieve over a far longer lifespan.

The trio were world changers. The rapid development of railways because of the sum total of the efforts of all three accelerated Britain's economic development, generating a far more mobile labour force that flocked to the new industrial cities, and allowed raw materials and finished goods to be moved far more cost effectively. Nearly 170 years later, Britain and the world owes them a huge debt of gratitude.

THE SYSTEM CONTRACTS

The final part of the original Cornwall Railway route, from Truro to Falmouth, was not opened until August 23, 1863, four years after Brunel's death.

The consortium of the GWR, Bristol & Exeter and the South Devon railways bought the cash-strapped West Cornwall Railway and converted it to mixed gauge. And so the Paddington to Penzance broad gauge, central to GWR folklore, was complete.

The first broad gauge freight trains ran on November 6, 1866, and passenger services started on March 1 the following year, with two through Paddington services each way from Penzance daily, the engine supplied by the South Devon Railway.

The consortium amalgamated as the Great Western Railway in 1876, with the West Cornwall system becoming part of that company.

However, despite this rare westwards expansion, Brunel's broad gauge was living on borrowed time.

On April 1, 1869, the broad gauge was taken out of use between Oxford and Wolverhampton and from Reading to Basingstoke. In August, the line from Grange Court to Hereford was converted from broad to standard, and the whole of the line from Swindon through Gloucester to South Wales was likewise adapted in May 1872. Mixed gauge was laid through Box Tunnel in 1875.

One last new broad gauge route was opened on June 1, 1877 – the St Ives branch in west Cornwall – although there was also a small extension at Sutton Harbour in Plymouth in 1879.

Once the GWR was in control of the whole line from London to Penzance

through a series of mergers and takeovers, it set about converting the remaining broad gauge tracks.

The last broad gauge service left Paddington station on Friday, May 20, 1892; the following Monday, trains from Penzance were operated by standard-gauge locomotives.

I have long drawn an analogy between the fate of Brunel's broad gauge and home video records in the 1980s. VHS led the market with its bulky cassette tapes, while those "in the know" testified that Betamax, which very much held second place in the market, was of a better quality.

A third entrant was V2000, which was widely praised by critics if only for its many advanced features, including smaller and longer tapes, also said to be of better quality.

However, VHS won the day hands down, because it had a head start through a superior marketing strategy, and V2000 was too late to jump on the bandwagon, and disappeared.

For V2000, read 7ft 0¼in gauge, and for VHS, Stephenson's gauge.

Broad gauge tracks were laid again at Swindon – to accommodate the vast amount of redundant broad gauge locomotives carriages and wagons that had nowhere left to run, and could only wait for the inevitable cutter's torch.

BELOW: Having set world record timings for passenger trains and bigger payloads, in theory Isambard Brunel's broad gauge should have become the norm for railways everywhere, but was doomed to fail because the narrower 4ft 8½in gauge had already claimed far more territory. A third of a century after the death of Brunel, his broad gauge locomotive and rolling stock were lined up waiting for the scrapman.

Lord of the Isles on display following the demise of the broad gauge system on which it ran. Like GWR pioneer *North Star*, it was offered to museums, but there were no takers, and both were scrapped.

ERASED FROM HISTORY?

The Times lamented the passing in its leader of May 23, 1892, as follows:

"A line which stands out from the rest by the adoption of a different gauge can neither give nor receive the amenities of an interchange of accommodation. It thus causes a breach of continuity where continuity would be of essential service, and if it persists in its policy of isolation it must do so at no small cost to itself and to its disobliged neighbours.

"This policy the Great Western Railway has at length finally given up, and the long-standing battle of the gauges is at an end. But the disappearance of the broad gauge is an event which we record with some regret and with some sense of loss. It is a triumph of utility, of common sense, of convenience; it is a concession to an irresistible foe; it has been long inevitable and it has come now as sooner or later it must have come. But the change thus made is by no means an unmixed benefit.

"The broad gauge had something more than a sentimental claim on our regard. It was a comfortable gauge to travel by. It allowed with safety a higher speed than can be attained by its rival. An express train on the old Great Western line conveyed its inmates not only more rapidly but more smoothly

than almost any other line in the country.

"The line, we must admit, cost more in construction; it was worked at greater expense. From the shareholders' point of view there can be no doubt which of the two systems was preferable. But its great champion, Brunel, had a soul above such base monetary considerations.

"His mind was in the grand style, and such too must be his work. But the views which found favour with him did not therefore commend themselves to intelligences cast in a different mould.

"His triumphs consequently were limited to the sphere within which he ruled supreme. There and there only could he give play to his inventive powers."

Only three broad gauge locomotives survived. *Lord of the Isles*, the most famous of Gooch's Iron Duke class, was exhibited at Chicago's World Fair in 1892, and at Earls' Court in 1897, the same year as the tracks on which it ran were ripped up. The pioneer *North Star* was also earmarked for preservation.

Disgracefully, both were scrapped because of a shortage of storage space at Swindon Works in January 1906. Only the driving wheels from *Lord of the Isles* survive, while the components from *North Star* were reassembled in 1923

into a non-working replica, which can be seen inside Swindon's STEAM – Museum of the Great Western Railway.

The only intact original broad gauge locomotive still with us is *Tiny*, an 0-4-0 vertical-boilered tank built for the South Devon Railway in 1868, for use on the Sutton Docks, and later transferred to Newton Abbot sheds. In 1927, it was preserved on display at the town's station, and is now inside the modern-day South Devon Railway's Buckfastleigh museum.

So we can visit Clifton Suspension Bridge, travel through Sonning Cutting and Box Tunnel, and marvel at the Royal Albert Bridge, along with other Brunel structures – but his magnificent broad gauge system has all but been wiped from history as if it never existed.

However, it is about as representative of Brunel and Gooch's magnificent broad gauge fleet as a Reliant Robin would be of the entire British motor car industry, Rolls-Royce and all.

In the preservation era, such losses to history have been somewhat rectified by the building of two new full-size broad gauge locomotives – *Iron Duke* and *Firefly* – which are currently based at the Great Western Society's Didcot Railway Centre.

The successor to the Great Western Railway – BR's Western Region – did its own thing again in Brunel fashion, when employing diesel hydraulic rather than diesel electric traction. Class 52 D1062 *Western Courier*, one of seven survivors of the Type 4 diesel-hydraulic locomotives built for the WR between 1961 and 1964, is pictured at Bridgnorth on the Severn Valley Railway. ROBIN JONES

INDEPENDENT TO THE LAST – AND BEYOND!

The GWR's 'go it alone' approach maybe inherited from the early days of Isambard Brunel and persisted into the British Railways era. At Nationalisation on January 1, 1948, the GWR became the Western Region (WR), and when BR published its 1956 Modernisation Plan, calling for the complete replacement of steam traction by diesel and electric locomotives, the region went its own way.

The WR opted for diesel hydraulic types to replace its legendary steam locomotives, while all other regions went for diesel electric.

Just as broad gauge had left the GWR isolated in much of the 19th century, so the WR found itself the odd man out again. When its diesel hydraulics visited other regions, the lack of standardisation meant drivers, fitters and maintenance men outside the Swindon empire were less familiar with them.

BR decided that in the name of standardisation the diesel hydraulics must go, and the last Class 52 Western Co-Cos were withdrawn in February 1977 – the same ideology that had eradicated the arguably superior broad gauge in favour of George Stephenson's gauge, derived from horse-drawn tramways.

A piece of Brunel broad gauge-era track still in use on Network Rail today. This section of rail helps support the platform at The Lakes Halt, at Earlswood, on the North Warwickshire Line between Birmingham and Stratford-upon-Avon. Opened by the GWR June 3, 1935, it brought visitors to Earlswood Lakes, the canal feeder reservoirs that formed part of the William James masterplan for an inter-city canal/rail system between Birmingham and London, as described in Chapter 5. The wheel turns full circle? ROBIN JONES